elementary PRINCIPLES

Six Foundational Principles of Ancient Jewish Christianity

D. THOMAS LANCASTER

elementary PRINCIPLES

Six Foundational Principles of Ancient Jewish Christianity

D. THOMAS LANCASTER

First Fruits of Zion is a 501(c)(3) registered nonprofit educational organization.

Printed in the United States of America

ISBN: 978-1-941534-03-8

Cover design: Avner Wolff

Quantity discounts are available on bulk purchases of this book for educational, fundraising, or event purposes. Special versions or book excerpts to fit specific needs are available from First Fruits of Zion. For more information, contact www.ffoz.org/contact.

First Fruits of Zion

Israel / United States / Canada

PO Box 649, Marshfield, Missouri 65706–0649 USA
Phone (417) 468–2741, www.ffoz.org

Comments and questions: www.ffoz.org/contact

ELEMENTARY PRINCIPLES_V6.INDD; 01-21-2016;

For Maria Anne
and for our children
Isaac, Gabriel, Simon, and Miriam.

May our Master receive them into the
school of his disciples.

CONTENTS

INTRODUCTION

Welcome to the club. This club has been called by many names: The Way, the Sect of the Nazarenes, the Disciples, the Christians, the Assembly, and, ultimately, the church. It has taken on many forms and expressed itself in a variety of ways as it has grown, evolved, and moved from culture to culture over the last two thousand years. It has multiplied, divided, morphed, and at some nasty points in history, cannibalized itself. Innumerable political, theological, and social divisions have fractured the club into sub-categories. In today's world, the club manifests itself primarily in the Roman Confession, the Orthodox Confession, and more than thirty-thousand Protestant denominations. In the face of all that history and conflict, the new initiate into the club might feel bewildered. Where should he or she join? Where does one even begin?

The place to begin, naturally, is the beginning. Regardless of which flavor of club you belong to, all club members have a common history and a common beginning.

In the beginning, the club was a Jewish club. All its members were originally Jewish. They practiced a religion which, in modern terms, can best be described as Messianic Judaism. Within a few decades, the charter members of the club took a vote, and they expanded the membership to include non-Jews, but that did not, at first, alter the fundamental Jewish nature of the institution.

To join the club, whether you were Jewish or Gentile, you had to consent to a few elementary principles. You had to agree to the club's manifestos and go through the club's initiation. This is a book about those basic first steps.

Nowadays, some chapters of this club require those undergoing initiation to learn a catechism. The word "catechism" comes from a Greek word (κατηχέω) that means "to teach orally." In Christian tradition, a catechism refers to a summary exposition of essential doctrines that a new initiate to the church must learn before he or she can be accepted into the church body.

In this book, I attempt to argue that "the elementary doctrine of Christ" presented in Hebrews 6:1–2 refers to an Apostolic-era initiation, like a catechism, into Jesus' school of disciples. Entering the club involved a series of beliefs the new initiate must confess and rites the new initiate must undergo. These rites of passage seem to be summarized as follows: "A foundation of repentance from dead works and of faith toward God, and of instruction about washings, the laying on of hands, the resurrection of the dead, and eternal judgment" (Hebrews 6:1–2). The six institutions that comprise the "elementary doctrine of Christ" in Hebrews 6:1–2 were the "basics" that the apostles and early believers taught to new disciples of Jesus. In that regard, the list can be read as essential prerequisite doctrines and practices incumbent upon the new believer.

The value of understanding the elementary principles should be self-evident. For the most part, the books of the New Testament assume that the reader is already a believer and therefore has already accepted the elementary doctrines, whatever they might be. For that reason, the New Testament does not bother introducing these foundational teachings, and one is left to discern the basics by inference. Even when the writer of the book of Hebrews lays out this list of basics, he does so only incidentally and without discussion. This book attempts to provide the definition of each elementary doctrine as well as discussion about each one.

Christian tradition provides its own catechisms and its own definitions for each of these elementary doctrines, but in this book I am interested in discovering how these basics of the faith would have been understood before Christianity left the Jewish matrix and evolved into a primarily Gentile religion. In other words, I want to know the elementary doctrine of Christ as the apostles themselves would have understood it within Judaism. This seems to me to be especially important when considering a text from the Epistle to the Hebrews, a word of exhortation written by a Jewish believer and addressed to Jewish believers. Unlike the Epistles of Paul, the book of Hebrews assumes a Jewish readership.

I first presented the contents of this book as Sabbath teachings at the Messianic Jewish congregation Beth Immanuel Sabbath Fellowship in Hudson, Wisconsin, in the year 2013. This printed edition contains several revisions and expansions to the material, but as in the original addresses, the teachings assume a readership already familiar with the theory of Messianic Judaism and the Jewish approach to Christianity. This is a book about a Messianic Jewish reading of the New Testament, Christianity, and the gospel.

Messianic Judaism starts with the assumption that Christianity was originally Jewish. Jesus, the apostles, and all the first disciples were practicing Jews who considered themselves part of Israel and the Jewish people. They did not envision themselves as the authors of a new religion; they considered themselves to be a sect within greater Judaism—a reformation movement inspired by the teachings of Jesus (Yeshua) of Nazareth and by their conviction that he is the long-promised Messiah King. They belonged to the sect of the Nazarenes, a first-century Jewish school of disciples centered around Yeshua. They did not hold Jesus or the gospel message in antithesis to the Law (Torah) of Moses. They upheld the words of Jesus:

> Do not think that I have come to abolish the Law or the Prophets; I have not come to abolish them but to fulfill them. For truly, I say to you, until heaven and earth pass away, not an iota, not a dot, will pass from the Law until all is accomplished. Therefore whoever relaxes one of the least of these commandments and teaches others to do the same will be called least in the kingdom of heaven, but whoever does them and teaches them will be called great in the kingdom of heaven. (Matthew 5:17–19)

Messianic Judaism is a branch of Judaism that honors Yeshua of Nazareth as Messiah and as the divine Son of God. The modern Messianic Jewish movement was born from Christian missionary efforts to evangelize Jews. In the late nineteenth century, Jewish believers in Jesus began to take ownership of their faith, eschewing Gentile Christian modes of worship and interpretation and working to establish an authentic Jewish expression of faith. In the 1960s and 1970s, the movement blossomed in the United States among young Jewish Christians of the Baby-Boom Generation. Since then it has outgrown its original chrysalis as a Jewish missionary effort and has begun to emerge as an independent sect of Judaism, much as the communities of the original apostles did.

Also, as those Apostolic-era Messianic communities did, Messianic Judaism includes a predominant number of Gentile participants. These Gentile Christians have entered the movement seeking a more historically authentic form of Christianity. In that regard, Messianic Judaism is no longer an exclusively Jewish movement (if it ever was), but instead it includes many "Messianic Gentiles" who, while not being Jewish, nevertheless have found a spiritual home in the Messianic synagogue. I am one of those Gentiles, but I pastor a Messianic Jewish congregation, pray in a Messianic Jewish synagogue, and teach with the Messianic Jewish ministry First Fruits of Zion. All this background information is necessary for the reader to understand the perspective from which I have written this book.

The teachings in this book belong to a much larger series of teachings on the Epistle to the Hebrews that I presented to the congregation of Beth Immanuel in 2013–2014. We spent more than a year in an ongoing string of expository sermons that meandered their way from one end of the book of Hebrews to the other. In the course of presenting these Sabbath sermons, I encountered the list in Hebrews 6:1–2. Originally I intended to quickly pass over the "elementary doctrine of Christ" without much comment, just as the writer of the book of Hebrews suggests when he says, "Let us leave the elementary doctrine of Christ and go on to maturity, not laying again" these basic teachings (Hebrews 6:1). After all, the list is not germane to the larger argument in the book of Hebrews. I covered the material in one quick sermon and told the congregation that I did not intend to take the time to explore the subject further, despite the fact that each elementary principle deserved a dedicated teaching.

The next day, by complete coincidence (so to speak), I received a sincere inquiry from one of First Fruits of Zion's readers, asking for an explanation of Hebrews 6:1–2. Furthermore, he suggested that our ministry should consider producing a teaching resource that would explain the elementary principles from a Jewish point of view. I considered the seeming serendipity of receiving this communication within twenty-four hours of declaring that I did not intend to teach the passage in detail. Over the next few days, several congregants contacted me with the same request. I took this to be direction from the LORD and agreed to dedicate the next several Sabbath sermons to the subject.

I attempted to provide the congregation with a historical, contextual explanation of the material, but I found it difficult to do so without first dispelling common misconceptions along the way. As a result, this book challenges several long-standing Christian interpretations, institutions, and matters of eschatology. It is not my intention to disparage Christian tradition; I am only interested in establishing a Messianic Jewish reading of the text. Nevertheless, I believe that the material has the potential to engage and energize traditional Christians and Christian churches, and I hope that the book will be read outside the small circles of Messianic Judaism. I hope that God might use this book to help reestablish the elementary doctrine of Christ and to initiate new disciples into the kingdom.

Needless to say, as a series of sermons transferred to print, this is not an academic work. I have intentionally attempted to keep it on a popular reading level, free of footnotes and documentation.

Chapter 1 introduces the list of six elementary principles in Hebrews 6:1–2 and offers a short summary of each. Chapter 2 draws on the work of Scot McKnight to compare the evangelical gospel message with the gospel proclaimed by Jesus and his disciples. Chapter 3 discusses the Messianic Jewish perspective on repentance as we explore the foundation of "repentance from dead works." In chapter 4, we consider the meaning of "faith toward God" and attempt to identify the unique perspective that the revelation of Yeshua brought to Jewish faith. Chapter 5 enters into the history behind Christian baptism by studying "instruction about washings" in the context of Jewish immersion rituals, finally concluding that the instruction about washings refers to an early type of catechism that new initiates completed prior to their immersion. Chapter 6 examines biblical and historical evidence to identify the ritual of "laying on of hands" as an investiture ceremony performed over new initiates into Jesus' school of disciples. Chapter 7 brings supporting evidence for these first four conclusions from early church literature, including the *Didache*, *Apostolic Constitutions*, and Justin Martyr. Chapter 8 challenges conventional Christian ideas about heaven as the place of our eternal home in order to introduce chapter 9's foundational teachings about "the resurrection of the dead." Chapter 10 concludes the list of elementary teachings with a quick look at apostolic eschatology pertaining to the "eternal judgment." The final chapter offers a few concluding thoughts and suggestions for implementation.

Thank you to the good people at Beth Immanuel who encouraged me to put this material together in the first place. Thank you to my friend and colleague Boaz Michael of First Fruits of Zion who asked me to assemble it into a book for publication through the ministry. Thank you to my wife and children who have now endured nearly fifteen years of my weekly Sabbath teachings. Thank you to all the *FFOZ Friends* who provide the financial support and spiritual encouragement necessary to make a book like this possible.

Whether you agree or disagree with the conclusions set forth in this book, I believe that you will at least find some inspiration along the way in your own devotion to Jesus and your own practice of the faith. Regardless of the differences in initiations and catechisms, ultimately, all disciples of Jesus share the unity of faith: "One Lord, one faith, one baptism, one God and Father of all, who is over all and through all and in all" (Ephesians 4:5–6). May every disciple of our holy Master Yeshua who reads and studies the basic teachings of Messiah in this book receive an abundant blessing for life and for peace, both in this world and in the one to come.

Maranatha!

D. Thomas Lancaster
HUDSON, WISCONSIN
17 ADAR I 5774

1

SIX BASIC TEACHINGS OF THE MESSIAH

> Everyone who lives on milk is unskilled in the word of righteousness, since he is a child. But solid food is for the mature, for those who have their powers of discernment trained by constant practice to distinguish good from evil. Therefore let us leave the elementary doctrine of Christ and go on to maturity, not laying again a foundation of repentance from dead works and of faith toward God, and of instruction about washings, the laying on of hands, the resurrection of the dead, and eternal judgment. And this we will do if God permits. (Hebrews 5:13–6:3)

Are you a spiritual person? A mature Christian? The apostles do not think that you are unless you have mastered the basic principles of the oracles of God. If you still need someone to teach you the elementary doctrine of Christ, you are unskilled in the Word of righteousness and still need milk. You are not yet ready for solid food.

The writer of the book of Hebrews wanted to present his readers with some exciting thoughts about Jesus. He wanted to start exploring some heady insights about the work of Messiah, his eternal priesthood, and the mysterious, mystical, priestly order of Melchizedek, but he felt frustrated because his readership seemed unprepared for these deeper, spiritual lessons. He wanted to go deep, but his readers were still shallow. They did not have the basics down. He wrote, "It is hard to explain, since you have become dull of hearing. For though by this time you ought to be teachers, you need someone to teach you again the basic principles of the oracles of God. You need milk, not solid food" (Hebrews 5:11–12).

GOT MILK?

The author of the book of Hebrews wanted to feed his readers meat and potatoes, but he feared that they might not be able to digest them. They were as yet spiritually immature, like children still at the breast, far past the age when they should have been weaned. It's as if he was saying, "I want to give you some heavy teaching, but you still need to learn the ABCs."

The Apostle Paul expressed a similar frustration in his Epistle to the Corinthians:

> But I, brothers, could not address you as spiritual people, but as people of the flesh, as infants in Christ. I fed you with milk, not solid food, for you were not ready for it. And even now you are not yet ready. (1 Corinthians 3:1–2)

Apparently, the Jewish readers of the Epistle to the Hebrews needed to spiritually grow more before they could begin to really grasp the deep things of Jesus—but hold on a minute. Is that really true? Were the readers of his epistle really "infants in Christ"?

The Epistle to the Hebrews contains some of the most difficult material in the whole New Testament. A careful reading of the book reveals multiple layers of complexity and sophisticated biblical allusions employing rabbinic methods of argumentation. For example, read the first two chapters. The writer assumed that his readership understood what he was writing, but he was writing at a level of biblical literacy that far surpasses our own today. He expected his readers to recognize and understand subtle allusions to numerous Old Testament passages. He bandied about quotations from the Torah, the Psalms, and the Prophets in a sort of apostolic shorthand to invoke whole concepts and inter-textual relationships. He employed rabbinic modes of exegesis and argumentation that required his readers to be well-studied and adept in those forms of discourse. So what did he mean by saying to his readers "You still need milk"?

If the Jewish believers in the Hebrews community still needed milk, and that kind of teaching was what the writer called "milk," then what are Christians today drinking? The stuff being fed to believers and passed off as deep, Christian education, I'm afraid, isn't even real milk; instead, it's the spiritual equivalent of baby formula. It's a series of formulas and dogmas that require no real biblical literacy and that never go deeper than a few centimeters.

SIX FOUNDATIONS

What was the spiritual "milk" that the apostles fed to new believers? The writer of the book of Hebrews refers to the milk—the baby stuff—as the elementary teachings about Messiah. Another way of saying that would be "the basics of Christian faith." Even better, and less anachronistic, we could call it "the basic teachings of the Messiah."

As I read Hebrews 6:1–2, I count six of these basic teachings. They are the first-century, Apostolic-era equivalent of Campus Crusade's Four Spiritual Laws—except that there are six of them. You might call this passage an apostolic catechism. The author of the book of Hebrews calls these doctrines "foundations." He lists six foundational teachings:

Therefore let us leave the elementary doctrine of Christ and go on to maturity, not laying again a foundation of [1] repentance from dead works and of [2] faith toward God, and of [3] instruction about washings, [4] the laying on of hands, [5] the resurrection of the dead, and [6] eternal judgment. (Hebrews 6:1–2)

1. Repentance from dead works
2. Faith toward God
3. Instruction about washings
4. The laying on of hands
5. The resurrection of the dead
6. Eternal judgment

Do we have a good handle on all these? Have we got this stuff down? We do not. I'm sorry to say that almost two thousand years later we have even less of a clue about these six foundations than the readers of the epistle possessed.

In this book, we are going to try to lay these foundations again. This is a book of milk. This book presents an introduction to the six foundational "basics of Christian faith" to make sure that we understand them. We are going to study them from a Messianic Jewish perspective because, after all, Christianity was still Jewish back then, and the Jewish writer of the Epistle to the Hebrews was writing to Jewish believers. Scholars recognize that all six foundational doctrines belong to the world of Jewish practice and Jewish theology. In view of that fact, we could call this study the six foundational "basics of Messianic Judaism." In those days, Christianity had not yet separated from its Jewish roots, and it functioned as a sect (or denomination) within larger Judaism.

This book consists of a collection of sermons about the six foundations that I originally delivered to my own Messianic Jewish and Gentile community of faith. Although I have written the book from a Messianic perspective with Messianic Jewish congregations in mind, I believe that the material will be pertinent to all Christians in all denominations because the six basic fundamentals are things that we all share in common. They represent our common origin in the teachings of the first-century apostles.

Let's take a brief overview of the six fundamental teachings of the Messiah.

1. REPENTANCE FROM DEAD WORKS

The book of Hebrews lists repentance from dead works as the first basic teaching of Christ. Protestants often read this one backwards to mean repentance from observing the rituals and ceremonies of Judaism. According to that opinion, the term "dead works" refers to the commandments in the Old Testament. In other words, "dead works" are the "works" of the Torah. It's not uncommon for a teacher or a pastor to explain the first foundational, elementary doctrine of Christ—the most basic teaching of Christianity—as repentance from keeping the Law. That is, repentance from works, because "no one is saved by works but only by grace through faith."

On the contrary, "dead works" is another name for sin, not for obedience to the Law. Paul says, "The wages of sin is death" (Romans 6:23). The Torah (Law) itself says, "I have set before you life and death, blessings and curses. Now choose life, so that you and your children may live" (Deuteronomy 30:19 NIV). Sin is the agent of death. Through sin, death came into the world.

We are thinking totally backwards if we suppose that one should repent from obeying God's commandments. What does repentance mean? It means to stop sinning, turn around, and start walking according to God's instructions. Moses taught it. The prophets taught it. And in the days of our Master, even the Pharisees taught it.

The writer of our epistle calls repentance an elementary teaching of Messiah because the gospel message started with a call to repentance. One might even say that repentance is the essential gospel message. The gospel story begins with John the Immerser, preparing "the Way," calling out, "Repent, for the kingdom of heaven is at hand" (Matthew 3:2). That consistent message runs through the teachings of Jesus and the whole New Testament.

Most evangelicals believe that the gospel message is, "Believe in Jesus, and you will go to heaven when you die." Is that what Jesus preached? Is that what Jesus told his twelve disciples to proclaim as he sent them out to preach? Did he say, "As you go, proclaim this message: 'Believe in Jesus, and you will go to heaven when you die'"? That's not what the Scripture says. Maybe that's what Jesus' teaching means, but the real message of the gospel that he told his disciples to proclaim was the same message that he had been teaching and that John had been teaching:

> John the Baptist came preaching in the wilderness of Judea, "Repent, for the kingdom of heaven is at hand." (Matthew 3:1–2)

> From that time Jesus began to preach, saying, "Repent, for the kingdom of heaven is at hand." (Matthew 4:17)

> These twelve Jesus sent out, instructing them, "... Proclaim as you go, saying, 'The kingdom of heaven is at hand.'" (Matthew 10:5–7)

Yes, repentance is an elementary teaching of Messiah. To teach that repentance from dead works means to turn away from God's Law is not only bizarre and backwards, I think it is satanic. Even the milk isn't being taught anymore. We're feeding our babies poison from the bottle.

2. FAITH TOWARD GOD

The foundational teaching of faith toward God seems obvious enough: you have to believe in God to be a Christian, right? *Faith* in God is not the same as *belief* in God. James, the brother of Jesus, says that even the demons believe, but assuredly the demons are not Christians. What is faith toward God?

As a fundamental teaching of the Messiah, faith toward God must be the kind of faith in God that Jesus taught. It is faith in the Father as revealed through the Son: "Faith is the assurance of things hoped for, the conviction of things not seen" (Hebrews 11:1). It's the assurance of the coming kingdom that we hope for, even though we do not yet see it in this world. In this respect, faith toward God is not as much *what* you believe as it is about *how* you believe.

The type of faith toward God that Jesus taught entails trusting in the Father's sovereignty, trusting that he is in control. And not only that; it is trusting that he punishes sin and rewards righteousness, whether in this life or in the next. This type of faith entails the fear of the LORD, because "without faith it is impossible to please him, for whoever would draw near to God must believe that he exists and that he rewards those who seek him" (Hebrews 11:6). It disturbs me to hear teaching about God that tries to undermine this principle. Grace-preachers love to quote Isaiah 64:6: "All our righteous deeds are like a polluted garment," and then they declare, "All our sins are forgiven by grace." As a result, many Christians believe in a God who does not reward righteousness or punish sin.

Surely it is true that we find forgiveness and reconciliation by the grace of God that he bestowed upon his Son Jesus. By the merit of our Master's suffering, we have the forgiveness of sins and hope for eternal life. But that does not, in any way, mean that God is no longer in the business of punishing sin and rewarding righteousness. True faith toward God trusts that God both punishes and rewards, whether in this life or in the next, and that he is in control—and more than that, that he is good. This is the God revealed to us through the Scriptures and the teaching of Jesus.

3. INSTRUCTION ABOUT WASHINGS

The book of Hebrews lists instruction about washings as the third basic teaching of the Messiah. Other English translations say "instruction about baptisms." Both translations are correct, because we derive the word "baptism" from the Greek word (*baptismo*) for "washing" and "immersing." Notice that the writer of the epistle did not say "instruction about baptism"; he said "instruction about baptisms."

In the days of the apostles, Jewish people knew about baptism. In those days, Jewish people in Jerusalem underwent a ceremonial immersion every time they entered the Temple. They immersed themselves to remove Levitical defilement. The Bible required people visiting the Temple in Jerusalem to go through a ceremonial immersion before they could enter God's house. Some people, such as the priests, immersed themselves every day.

Even today, some pious Jews immerse themselves prior to Sabbaths and festivals as a remembrance of the Temple. To prepare for marriage, both the bride and the groom go through a baptism for ritual purity on the night before their wedding day. Married women undergo a similar immersion at least once a month. Those who wash the dead in preparation for burial go through a baptism-immersion before and after the ceremonial washing of the corpse. They wash the corpse to prepare it for the resurrection. Judaism employs many different types of "baptisms," which is why the English Standard Version avoids the word "baptism" with all its Christian, sacramental associations and translates the Greek *baptismo* as "washings."

In keeping with the Jewish mode of immersion for ceremonial purification, John the Baptist introduced a baptism of repentance. He told people to confess their sins, repent, and immerse themselves. The apostles called on people to confess their sins and immerse themselves in the name of Jesus.

When Christianity broke free from her Jewish moorings, the ceremony of baptism evolved into a sacramental rite, and the church abandoned the Jewish form of the immersion ritual. The Anabaptists of the Reformation Era attempted to restore the original Jewish version of the ritual, but even among Protestants, to this very day, Christians debate the significance, symbolism, and procedure of baptism. The divide over baptism continues to segment Christianity and polarize churches.

In light of the baptism debates, one might assume that instruction about washings refers to instructions on how to administer the ceremony of baptism. On the contrary, that cannot be what the book of Hebrews was talking about here. Why would the apostles need to give Jewish believers instructions about how to conduct immersions? It makes no sense to think that this elementary principle of faith in Messiah could have been about how to use a mikvah (ceremonial bathing pool). Every Jew knew how to conduct an immersion.

Instead, "the instruction" refers to the basic teachings of Jesus that the apostles presented to people before immersing them. One might think of the instruction as an early catechism. In the nineteenth century, a first-century "instruction about baptisms" that the apostolic community had created for new Gentile Christians to study prior to undergoing baptism was actually rediscovered. The document is titled *The Instruction of the Master to the Gentiles through the Twelve Apostles*. It is called the *Didache* for short, which means *The Instruction*. It consists of a basic course of apostolic instruction in the teachings of our Master that a person learned prior to undergoing baptism into the name of Jesus. We could think of it as a *Discipleship 101* course. The apostles considered that type of instruction before baptism to be elementary—the milk fed to new believers.

4. THE LAYING ON OF HANDS

The institution of the laying on of hands also comes from the Torah and from Jewish practice. In the Temple, a man laid his hands on the head of the animal he was about to sacrifice so that it would be accepted and identified on his behalf. In the Torah,

Moses laid hands on Joshua to install him as the new leader. Several other examples occur in the Old Testament.

The Jewish sages and teachers of Torah in the Apostolic Era also used the ritual to confer discipleship. A sage laid hands on his disciples in order to ordain them as teachers. The rabbis speak of a chain of tradition and ordination by which one generation passes the torch of Torah to the next. This is what the laying on of hands means in this context. It refers to the Jewish custom of initiating a new disciple.

For example, when Timothy first became a disciple of Jesus, the council of elders in his congregation laid hands upon him, and they prophesied over him. Paul said to Timothy, "Do not neglect the gift you have, which was given you by prophecy when the council of elders laid their hands on you" (1 Timothy 4:14). In the same epistle, Paul warned Timothy, "Do not be hasty in the laying on of hands, nor take part in the sins of others; keep yourself pure" (1 Timothy 5:22). In other words, "Don't be too quick to accept new disciples into the fold," or, perhaps, "Don't be too quick to appoint elders in the congregations." I think both interpretations work.

The laying on of hands signifies entrance into discipleship. It symbolizes an investment of Jesus' identity through the power and authority of his name. The apostles based it on a common Jewish practice that appears in the Torah. And it is milk; it is basic stuff—again, *Christianity 101*.

5. THE RESURRECTION OF THE DEAD

The foundational teaching of the resurrection of the dead simply means that there will be a resurrection. The doctrine has implications for us now, before death, and ramifications for us after death. The teaching of the resurrection of the dead includes discussion on who gets resurrected, on what criteria, when, and so forth. Jews in the first century hotly debated these questions. The Sadducees (who did not believe in a resurrection) hated the followers of Jesus primarily because the disciples of Jesus championed faith in the resurrection.

Traditional Jews consider a firm faith in the resurrection of the dead as fundamental to Judaism. Maimonides calls it one of the thirteen basic principles of Jewish faith. How much more so should we consider it to be a basic principle of faith for Messianic Judaism and Christianity?

I am astonished at how Christian teachers neglect and ignore the doctrine of the resurrection of the dead. They cannot reconcile it with the popular view of an eternal home in heaven. Despite our allegiance to the resurrected Jesus, we ignore the doctrine of resurrection, shove it under the table, and hide it in the closet. You will hear plenty of sermons about going to heaven and spending eternity in glory, but no one talks much about the hope of the resurrection. No one understands it. It seems like an embarrassment to modern man, as if the modern thinker is too sophisticated for such a primitive Hebrew superstition. We talk happily about going to heaven to be with Grandma, but the whole expectation of a literal, physical resurrection of the dead seems pretty murky. Nevertheless, every Easter, Christians gather to revel in the resurrection of Jesus.

Why do we have all this confused ambiguity about something so central to Christian faith? The doctrine of the resurrection of the dead should be a basic assumption. It is milk—something so fundamental to Christian belief that we should not need to explain it to people who call themselves Christians.

6. ETERNAL JUDGMENT

The final foundational doctrine in the series of six is the eternal judgment. It refers to the Pharisaic belief that we will all receive our comeuppance (or our reward) for how we lived, not just in this world but primarily in the next world—the next life. The doctrine of eternal judgment teaches that God will distribute divine punishment and divine reward to human beings in the afterlife. This world is merely a vestibule for the World to Come, and a person should prepare himself (or herself) in the vestibule so that he (or she) will be ready to enter the banquet hall. Repent now; work hard to enter into the eternal rest of Messiah, because there is an eye that sees and an ear that hears, and all your deeds are written in a book.

The doctrine of the eternal judgment entails the belief that every soul will stand before the judgment, that the heavenly court will open books of judgment, and that ultimately everyone will receive a verdict and find his name recorded either in the Book of Life or the book of death: the eternal verdict. Belief in the final, eternal judgment permeates all the teaching of Jesus and the New Testament. It was another of the foundational beliefs of Apostolic-era believers. And it is milk. It is basic stuff. Just the elementary principles.

THE BASIC GOSPEL

On closer examination, it turns out that the six doctrines sketch out the good news of the gospel. They call us to follow Jesus, enter the kingdom of heaven, and receive the final reward.

1. **Repentance**: Repent in the name of Jesus; turn away from sin; turn back to God's instruction for your life, because the kingdom is at hand.
2. **Faith toward God**: You are saved by grace through faith, and you must express your faith toward God by living it out.
3. **Instruction about washings**: Therefore, as a symbol of your repentance and your entrance into the kingdom, be immersed in the name of Jesus. Before you do that, however, you should learn some of the teachings of Jesus so that you understand the life to which you are committing yourself.
4. **Laying on of hands**: After your immersion, enter into the ranks of discipleship under the authority of the elders of your local congregation as they invest you with the laying on of hands.
5. **Resurrection of the dead**: As a disciple, you will live out the life of the resurrected Messiah now as you eagerly anticipate your own resurrection.
6. **Eternal judgment**: After the resurrection, you will face eternal judgment. If you are in Messiah, having complied with steps one through five, you will find forgiveness and pardon and entrance into eternal life.

These six doctrines outline the response that a person should have toward the gospel message. This is the milk of the Word—the basic stuff. I am astonished when I look at this simple gospel protocol as recorded in the New Testament and realize how very few points of contact still exist between these six basic principles of Messiah and the conventional message that passes for the gospel in today's churches. The writer of the book of Hebrews says, "Therefore let us leave the elementary doctrine of Christ and go on to maturity. … And this we will do if God permits" (Hebrews 6:1–3). God permitting, we will do so as well.

2
THE EVANGELICAL GOSPEL

Today I am a Gentile pastor and educator in Messianic Judaism, but I was not always Messianic. I grew up in a devout evangelical Christianity attending Sunday school, Sunday morning service, Sunday evening service, after-school parochial clubs, Wednesday night Bible studies, Vacation Bible School, and numerous other events. It did not take me too long to figure out the rules. I learned that there were two types of people in the world: those going to hell, and those going to heaven. To qualify for the first group, one need do nothing at all. Everyone is going to hell. To qualify for the second group, one need only accept Jesus into his heart as his personal Lord and Savior.

Once a person accepts Jesus into his heart, he becomes a Christian, and his new job is to save as many people from hell as possible by witnessing to them about the gospel, trying to convince them to also accept Jesus into their hearts.

The evangelical gospel is short, sweet, and simple, but the gospel according to Matthew is twenty-eight chapters long. The gospel according to Mark has sixteen chapters. The gospel according to Luke goes on for twenty-four chapters. The gospel according to John contains twenty-one chapters. All these presentations of the good news are fairly substantial and require a moderate degree of literacy. The gospel according to evangelicals, on the other hand, presents a much shorter version of the good news: "Jesus died to save you from your sins. Believe in him for the forgiveness of sins, and you will go to heaven when you die." Much more concise and to the point than those cumbersome biographies in the New Testament.

In my early twenties, I encountered Messianic Judaism. It deeply challenged my evangelical interpretation of the gospel. For the first time, I learned to read the Gospels from a Jewish perspective. I discovered a gospel message that had very little to do with going to heaven but a great deal to do with something called the kingdom of heaven. It turns out that the term "kingdom of heaven" does not refer to going to heaven, it refers to the coming Messianic Era, a golden age predicted by all the prophets in which God will gather his people Israel, restore them to their land, and place his Messiah as King over them. Actually, this is the main message of the gospel. Somehow, despite attending Sunday school, Sunday morning service, Sunday evening service, after-school parochial clubs, Wednesday night Bible studies, and Vacation Bible School, I missed that part of the good news.

EVANGELICALISM

Evangelicals are a certain breed of Protestants. The word "evangelical" is based on the Greek word *evaggelion* (εὐαγγέλιον), which means "good news." It's the same word our English Bibles translate as "gospel." In that sense, to be an evangelical means to be a gospel preacher.

I have a great deal of respect for my evangelical roots. I regard Billy Graham as a prophet of our generation. His message has impacted thousands and thousands of lives, ushering them from the kingdom of darkness to the kingdom of light.

> Just as I am, without one plea but that thy blood was shed for me.

I stand in awe of evangelicalism. The modern Messianic Jewish movement emerged from evangelicalism. Without evangelicalism, Messianic Judaism would not be here today. Ironically, my evangelical background led me to explore Messianic Judaism as a natural consequence of evangelical teachings about the authority of the Bible.

In terms of church history, evangelicals and their particular expression of the gospel message appeared fairly recently. Evangelicalism is one of the youngest siblings in the family of Christianity. The evangelical movement began in the early eighteenth century in Europe, mostly in England, under the preaching of John Wesley and spread in America under the fiery preaching of George Whitfield and Jonathan Edwards. The movement caught fire in the United States during a series of revivals called the Great Awakening in the eighteenth and nineteenth centuries. Evangelists such as D. L. Moody brought thousands to faith. In our own day and age, the great Billy Graham carried the legacy forward with his famous stadium-packed crusade meetings.

Today nearly one hundred million Christians identify themselves as evangelicals. That's only a small percentage of the billion-plus Christians in the world, but the United States has a large and vocal concentration of evangelicals. Roughly twenty-five million Americans identify themselves as evangelical.

The genius of evangelicalism introduced a personalization of the gospel. Prior to the evangelical movement, most of Christianity operated on a more institutional level. From the institutional perspective, individuals are not saved; rather, the church is saved, and individuals access salvation by accessing the church, either by consenting to its creeds or by participating in its sacraments. This formula does not call for a great deal of personal commitment or personal relationship, nor does it encourage personal spiritual growth for most. The average Christian leaves his religion in the hands of the professional clerical class and lets the leaders deal with the Scriptures and figure out the details. In the mainstream institutional approach, a good Christian does his part by going through the sacraments and attending church services.

The evangelical movement calls for individuals to make a personal decision to follow Christ. It emphasizes that every person must develop a relationship with God and ultimately stand accountable before him. It calls on people to have an individualized experience of salvation, independent of affiliation with an institutional church.

These ideas bring us a lot closer to the Master's original call to discipleship. Jesus called individuals, telling them, "Take up your cross, and follow me" (Mark 8:34 NLT). He called individuals, warning them to count the cost of discipleship before rashly committing to it. He challenged individuals to repent of their sin: "Go and sin no more" (John 8:11 NLT). He saw that the institutional-level transformation of the nation of Israel had to happen on the individual level of repentance.

THE EVANGELICAL GOSPEL

All that sounds fabulous, but modern evangelicalism poses one problem. At least in recent times, the gospel taught by evangelicals is not really the same good news that Jesus taught, that Paul taught, or that any of the apostles taught. You will never read in the Gospel of Matthew that our Master went up on a hill, sat down, and began to teach his disciples, "Believe in me for the forgiveness of your sins so that you will go to heaven when you die." Nor did Paul or the apostles.

As a young evangelical and the son of an evangelical pastor who grew up in an evangelical church, I found this dichotomy to be extremely frustrating. It resulted in an acute crisis of faith for me around the age of sixteen. I remember reading the Gospels and throwing my Bible across the room in frustration. I could not find the evangelical gospel message on the lips of Jesus or in the writings of the apostles. Instead, the message Jesus and the disciples taught sounded to me a lot like legalism. Or what we called legalism anyway. It sounded works-based and legalistic. My frustration came from the disconnect that I encountered between the words and teachings of Jesus and the apostles and the good-news message I learned from evangelicalism: believe in Jesus for the forgiveness of sins so that you will go to heaven when you die.

I do not mean to diminish that truth, but like a man on trial, I swear to tell the whole truth and nothing but the truth, and that message does not present the *whole* truth. It is a part of the gospel, but it is not the *whole* gospel.

KING JESUS GOSPEL

Evangelical thinker, seminary teacher, and writer Scot McKnight recently released a book he titled *The King Jesus Gospel.* My colleague Boaz Michael recommended it to me. I bought a copy and made my way through it. It's a quick read. It has one basic premise: the gospel message taught by evangelicals today is not the original gospel message taught by Jesus and the apostles. McKnight's premise is probably not news to anyone in the Messianic Jewish movement, but it is surprising to hear it from an evangelical leader. Not only that, but McKnight rallies support for his position from other big names like N.T. Wright and Dallas Willard. Essentially, the book says that evangelicalism has mistaken the message of salvation for the message of the gospel. The two are not the same. Evangelicals do not teach the gospel, they teach salvation. Evangelicals should be called "soterical s," which means "salvationists." They are not teaching the good news of the Bible, they are teaching a formula for attaining personal salvation. As a result, the church has developed into what McKnight calls a "salvation culture" instead of a "gospel culture."

McKnight points out that this gospel of a personal salvation message has no real use for the Old Testament. It has no use for the historical story of Israel. Those are vestigial elements that can be left out because they are not essential to message of belief in Jesus so that you can go to heaven. In that sense, the evangelical gospel is not really about replacement theology as much as displacement theology. It displaces Israel and the Jewish people. It has no use for them.

Neither does the personal salvation message have any real use for the second coming and the advent of the kingdom of heaven (the Messianic Era) except to scare people into accepting the salvation message before their time runs out. The evangelical gospel of salvation has no real need for a restored Israel, a literal kingdom on earth, a resurrection, a new Jerusalem, the Torah going forth from Zion, or any of the prophecies of the kingdom of heaven.

McKnight goes on to identify what he considers to be a more biblical expression of the full gospel message, which he develops from 1 Corinthians 15 and from the church creeds. That's not exactly the direction I would have gone if I had been writing the book. He correctly diagnoses the problem, but the way he phrases the correction—well, it's not quite the way we would say it in Messianic Judaism. He summarizes the gospel as the conclusion and fulfillment of Israel's story. That summary cuts out the kingdom and continues to perpetrate a replacement-theology mindset. McKnight's otherwise excellent critique still misses the larger prophetic aspects of the gospel such as the story of Israel's national redemption and the kingdom of heaven on earth.

THE FULL GOSPEL

Distilled to a simple one-liner, the gospel message Jesus of Nazareth taught was "Repent, for the kingdom of heaven is at hand." What does that mean?

Try this gospel message on for size:

> Repent, because the Messianic Age is near. How near is it? So near that the Messiah has already been identified: Jesus of Nazareth, a son of David attested to by God with mighty works and wonders and signs that God did through him. He was delivered up according to the definite plan and foreknowledge of God, crucified and killed by the hands of lawless men, but God raised him up, loosing him from the pangs of death, because it was not possible for him to be held by death. He has ascended to the right hand of the Father, and having received the Holy Spirit, has poured it out upon his disciples. Therefore, repent from your sins, turn to God, be immersed for the name of Jesus the King to become his disciple, and you will receive the forgiveness of your sins and the gift of the Holy Spirit. When he comes again, he will bring the Messianic Era and establish the kingdom of heaven and everything that it entails. He will defeat the enemies of Israel, bring an end to the exile of the Jewish people, and restore the kingdom to Israel, just as the prophets predicted. At that time, God will raise his disciples from the dead to join him, just as he raised Jesus from the dead. After the kingdom, then comes the final judgment, when every person who ever lived must stand before the throne of judgment. The names of those who have obeyed King Jesus and trusted him for the forgiveness of their sins are recorded in the Book of Life along with the names of the saints. This promise is for Jewish people and for their children and

> for all who are far off, for everyone whom the LORD our God calls to himself.

That's how I would put it.

Actually, that's basically how Peter put it the first time he presented the gospel on the day of Shavuot (Pentecost) in Acts 2. It must have been a powerful way to present the gospel, because those who received his word, some three thousand souls, joined the disciples that day and underwent immersion in the name of Jesus.

I admit, this version of the gospel is a lot more difficult to communicate, and it might not fit on a tract, but this version of the gospel is the real deal. This is the amplified version of the words "Repent, for the kingdom of heaven is at hand."

PARTIAL CONVERTS

I'm not saying that evangelicals are wrong, and neither is Scot McKnight, N.T. Wright, or Dallas Willard. They only say that today's evangelicalism presents an incomplete gospel. The evangelical gospel is not wrong, but it is missing some important parts, such as radical repentance, discipleship, redemption from exile, the restoration of Israel, and the kingdom of heaven.

That means that we have millions and millions of professing Christians today who do not know the real gospel. We have a mission field among the evangelicals in our own backyard, not to mention among other Protestants and sacramental segments of Christianity. It appears that most of the billion or so Christians on planet earth do not know the original gospel. They know parts of it. A piece here. A piece there. But the same anti-Jewish theology that severed Christianity from Judaism in the second century has severed Christians today from the full message of the gospel.

A gospel message that does not preach repentance is not the full gospel. A gospel message that does not preach immersion is not a full gospel message. A gospel message that does not preach discipleship to Jesus is not a full gospel message. A gospel message that does not preach the kingship of Jesus, including subjection to his lordship, is not a full gospel message. A gospel message that does not teach the restoration of Israel and of the Jewish people is not a full gospel message. A gospel message that does not teach the coming kingdom of heaven on earth is not a full gospel message. A gospel message that does not teach the physical, literal resurrection of the dead is not a full gospel message.

Ironically, when the gospel is reduced to merely the salvation message, it becomes so neutered that one wonders if it even has the power to save. It calls people to ask Jesus to forgive their sins, but does it call for people to renounce those same sins and surrender their lives to the King? A partial proclamation of the gospel produces partial converts, not disciples. The church is full of lukewarm Christians, neither hot nor cold, who love to sing and worship and go through the religious motions on a Sunday morning but have never really experienced the life-changing conversion to which the gospel calls us. They have never really surrendered the authority over their lives to our Master. Does such a gospel save?

JESUS AND THE RICH YOUNG MAN

Our Master rarely spoke about personal salvation. His gospel of repentance and the nearness of the kingdom included the concept of salvation, but he rarely singled it out. On certain occasions, however, someone asked him directly about the matter. For example, we see an exchange he had in Luke 18:18–22 with a rich young nobleman. The young man asked, "What must I do to inherit eternal life?"

When I was a young evangelical, this is one of those passages that frustrated me, frightened me, and inspired me to fling my Bible across the room. Here was a guy asking Jesus point blank, "What must I do to inherit eternal life?"

Jesus answered him, "You know the commandments. You shall not commit adultery. You shall not murder. You shall not steal. You shall not give false testimony. Honor your father and your mother." And so forth.

What kind of answer was this? As a young evangelical, I wanted to hear him say, "Trust in me for the forgiveness of sins." Instead he gave the man what seemed to me to be legalism: "Keep the commandments."

In the story, the young man replied, "I have kept all these from my youth."

Jesus said, "If you want to have treasure in heaven"—that is, merit with God—"then sell everything you have and give it to the poor. Then come follow me."

This does not sound like the gospel of salvation at all. Jesus is asked, "What must I do to be saved?" and he speaks about commandments and merit.

We used to explain, "Well, he was simply showing the young man not to trust in his own righteousness." That's not what it says, is it? I hardly think it fair to suppose that Jesus answered the man sarcastically or gave him a dishonest answer in order to cause him to think his way to the realization that what he really needed to do was just trust in Jesus.

THE NARROW DOOR

Another troubling example of Jesus' own directives for attaining salvation occurred when someone asked him directly, "Lord, will those who are saved be few?" (Luke 13:23). He replied, "Strive to enter through the narrow door. For many, I tell you, will seek to enter and will not be able" (Luke 13:24).

This does not sound like the evangelical message of salvation. According to the evangelical perspective, the answer to that question is that many will be saved. Whole stadiums full will be saved, and their salvation requires very little effort. All people need to do is trust in Jesus for the forgiveness of sins. Receive him into their heart. Believe. There is no striving to enter through a narrow door. There is no striving at all, really. Just accepting. Just receiving. Just making a decision to receive Jesus as your personal Lord and Savior. No seeking to enter and then finding oneself on the wrong side of the door.

But listen to how Jesus' teaching continues:

> When once the master of the house has risen and shut the door, and you begin to stand outside and to knock at the door, saying, "Lord, open to us," then he will answer you, "I do not know where you come from." Then you will begin to say, "We ate and drank in your presence, and you taught in our streets." But he will say, "I tell you,

> I do not know where you come from. Depart from me, all you workers of evil!" (Luke 13:25–27)

Why doesn't he say, "Depart from me, you people who did not receive me as your personal Savior"? Why doesn't he say, "Depart from me, you who have not confessed your sins and accepted me into your hearts"? Why does he say, "Depart from me, all you workers of evil!" Once again, it sounds so legalistic. Where's the grace?

> In that place there will be weeping and gnashing of teeth, when you see Abraham and Isaac and Jacob and all the prophets in the kingdom of God but you yourselves cast out. (Luke 13:28)

We could look at many other examples. Suffice to say, Jesus' teaching is not the evangelical gospel of salvation.

THE BASIC PRINCIPLES

Scot McKnight asks, "Did Jesus preach the gospel?" That depends on how you define the gospel. If you believe that the gospel is simply believing in Jesus so that you will go to heaven when you die, then no, he did not preach that. If the gospel means a message of repentance, faith, discipleship, and, ultimately, resurrection and the final redemption in the kingdom of heaven, then yes, he certainly did preach the gospel.

The problem, once again, as McKnight diagnoses it, is that the evangelical gospel is not the good news of the gospel. This might be new information to Scot McKnight's readers, but it is certainly not new information to Messianic Judaism.

Messianic Judaism brings us many gifts, not the least of which is this opportunity to reclaim the authentic, biblical good news. The sad thing is that we should not need to relearn the gospel. We should be able to move on to the solid meat of the Word and to see the deeper mysteries in the gospel:

> For though by this time you ought to be teachers, you need someone to teach you again the basic principles of the oracles of God. You need milk, not solid food. (Hebrews 5:12–13)

Hebrews 6:1–2 quickly lays out six principles that the author of that epistle considers to be just milk—the baby stuff—for new believers. He calls them "the basic principles of the oracles of God" and "the elementary doctrine of the Messiah." They are foundations on which the gospel message stands. If we want to understand the authentic gospel taught by Jesus and the apostles, we need to have these basic elementary teachings firmly in place. When understood together, the six principles do present the message of personal salvation.

For the remainder of this book, we are going to invest some time into these basic principles of the oracles of God, the elementary doctrine of Messiah, which are foundations for the message of the gospel and for personal salvation:

> Therefore let us leave the elementary doctrine of Christ and go on to maturity, not laying again a foundation of repentance from dead works and of faith toward God, and of instruction about washings, the laying on of hands, the resurrection of the dead, and eternal judgment. (Hebrews 6:1–2)

Unlike the recipients of the book of Hebrews, for our part, we are going to spend some time learning the elementary doctrine of the Messiah. We are going to lay once again a foundation of repentance from dead works, a foundation of faith toward God, a foundation of instruction about immersions, a foundation of the laying on of hands, a foundation of the resurrection of the dead, and a foundation of eternal judgment.

3
REPENTANCE FROM DEAD WORKS

> Let us leave the elementary doctrine of Christ and go on to maturity, not laying again a foundation of repentance from dead works. (Hebrews 6:1)

Jesus told a parable about the kingdom. In the parable, a king was hosting a wedding banquet for his son, and he invited everyone. The king represents the LORD. The king's son is, of course, the Messiah. And the banquet represents the kingdom of heaven, that is, the Messianic Era. When the banquet was ready, the king sent his servants out to invite the guests. He said, "Go therefore to the main roads and invite to the wedding feast as many as you find" (Matthew 22:9). The servants went out to the streets and gathered everyone they found, both high and low, both bad and good. The king's wedding hall filled with guests, all dressed in festive attire.

Then the king came in to greet the guests. He saw one man at the table wearing his street clothes. He had not dressed for the occasion. He was not wearing a wedding garment. The king said to him, "Friend, how did you get in here without a wedding garment?" (Matthew 22:12). The underdressed man had no answer. He could not think of a single excuse to justify his presence at the banquet in common clothing. Then the king said to the attendants, "Bind him hand and foot and cast him into the outer darkness. In that place there will be weeping and gnashing of teeth" (Matthew

22:13). Jesus explained, "For many are called, but few are chosen" (Matthew 22:14).

What does it mean to come to the banquet without wedding clothes? Before we can answer that, we need a bigger picture of the gospel.

A BIGGER PICTURE OF THE GOSPEL

In the previous chapter, we took a look at evangelicalism and the evangelical gospel. As a recovering evangelical myself, I wrote about my own misgivings and personal struggles with evangelicalism and the evangelical salvation message. We saw that the evangelical gospel is not the same good news that was taught by Jesus and the apostles. It presents one part of that message, but only part of it—specifically the part about salvation and eternal destinies. The evangelical gospel is about believing in Jesus and going to heaven when you die. This was not the good news predicted by the prophets, announced by John the Immerser, proclaimed by Jesus of Nazareth, and broadcast by Jesus' apostles.

The biblical good news is much broader, rooted in the Torah, the Prophets, and the Scriptures, and it is all about the people of Israel, the house of David, the land of Israel, the end of exile, the final redemption, and the kingdom of heaven.

This realization requires a monumental paradigm shift that has to happen if we want to truly receive the message of the kingdom that Jesus of Nazareth taught. We must broaden our definition of the gospel. A good first step toward that goal involves learning the elementary doctrine of Christ:

> Therefore let us leave the elementary doctrine of Christ and go on to maturity, not laying again a foundation of repentance from dead works and of faith toward God, and of instruction about washings, the laying on of hands, the resurrection of the dead, and eternal judgment. And this we will do if God permits. (Hebrews 6:1–3)

In this chapter, we will learn the first one on the list: "repentance from dead works." This first principle is nothing more than the basic message of repentance, the first step of the message of the kingdom. It is the good news that Jesus and the apostles preached: repent, because the Messianic Era is near.

REPENTANCE FROM JUDAISM

Repentance means to turn away from sin and start obeying God. Real repentance is the first step of the gospel, both in regard to presenting the good news of the kingdom and in regard to receiving the good news of the kingdom.

An astonishing number of Bible teachers completely misunderstand what Hebrews 6:1 means by repentance from dead works. According to many Bible teachers, repentance from dead works means turning away from Judaism. The dead works, they say, are works of the Law. According to this opinion, they are called dead works because they consist of legalism, and they can never earn us eternal life. Those who trust in them will be damned; therefore, they are dead works.

In my opinion, this interpretation suggests an incredible, supernatural, spiritual blindness that I would go so far as to characterize as diabolical. This interpretation fits hand in glove with the common Christian reading of the book of Hebrews, namely that the book of Hebrews was written by Paul to warn Jewish Christians from slipping back into Judaism and Torah observance. According to that interpretation, the first, most basic, elementary teaching of the Messiah was to renounce the Torah and the religion of the Jews. Therefore, one who keeps any of the Torah's so-called ceremonial commandments or participates in the Torah's institutions (such as the Sabbath, the calendar, the festivals, the dietary laws, the Levitical laws, the purity laws, the sacrifices, and the Temple) has not even taken the simple, most fundamental first step of the gospel. He has missed the number-one, elementary teaching of the Messiah—namely that the Torah is a book of dead works, and one must turn away from it.

That conventional interpretation of repentance from dead works is difficult to square with the teaching of Jesus, which says just the opposite:

> Do not think that I have come to abolish the Law or the Prophets; I have not come to abolish them but to fulfill

> them. For truly, I say to you, until heaven and earth pass away, not an iota, not a dot, will pass from the Law until all is accomplished. Therefore whoever relaxes one of the least of these commandments and teaches others to do the same will be called least in the kingdom of heaven, but whoever does them and teaches them will be called great in the kingdom of heaven. (Matthew 5:17–19)

DEAD WORKS

If repentance from dead works does not mean turning away from God's Law, as many teachers suppose, what does it really mean? It means repentance from sin. From an apostolic and Jewish perspective, "dead works" are sins.

The sages considered human mortality to be the consequence of sin. The Torah says, "Each one shall be put to death for his own sin" (Deuteronomy 24:16), and every man "died for his own sin" (Numbers 27:3). The rabbis explain that "Satan, the evil inclination, and the angel of death are all one." Likewise, the rabbis declared, "There is no death without sin, for it is written [in Ezekiel 18:20], 'The soul who sins shall die.'"

Our Master and the apostles firmly equated sin and death. "Sin when it is fully grown brings forth death" (James 1:15). "The wages of sin is death" (Romans 6:23). Death came into the world "through sin, and so death spread to all men because all sinned" (Romans 5:12), and sin "leads to death" (Romans 6:16). Paul refers to the sin-equals-death equation as "the law of sin and death" (Romans 8:2). You may have heard of Murphy's Law: everything that can go wrong will. The law of sin and death states: the wages of sin is death.

THE FIRST STEP

Repentance from sin is the first step to receiving the good news of Messiah and the kingdom of heaven and the first foundation upon which the good news is built. The gospel message is essentially a message of repentance. When preachers teach the gospel without a call to repent from sin, they are not teaching the good news. Their message is not founded on the basic teachings of the Messiah.

Sin is an obstacle to relationship with God. Sin causes the LORD to turn away from us, both as individuals and as a people. Sin delays the redemption. Sin brings exile. Sin breaks our communion with God, and it bars us from the redemption and the Messianic Era. Sin begets death in this world and in the next.

WHAT IS SIN?

What is sin? The Bible defines sin as transgression of the commandments of the Torah. Specifically, those commandments that apply to you. Not all the commandments in God's law apply equally to everyone. Some commandments apply only to men; some apply only to women. Some apply only to Levitical priests; some apply only to laymen. Some apply only to Jewish people; some apply to everyone.

When I grew up, we simple Bible-believing, fundamentalist-leaning, evangelical types defined sin as violation of the Ten Commandments and of course all the New Testament injunctions plus a few additional prohibitions of our own. Those additional sins included smoking, drinking, dancing, gambling, dating, and going to movies (especially R-rated movies).

I used to make fun of those puritanical rules, but over the years, I have come to see the great wisdom in the old fundamentalist prohibitions on smoking, drinking, dancing, gambling, and movies. Those rules were fences around real sin, not unlike fences imposed by the sages and rabbis to protect the Jewish people from violating the commandments. It's not that any of those activities is in itself specifically a sin, but every one of them opens a portal to sin, addiction, or sexual immorality. These fundamentalist prohibitions were not so much about puritanical values as they were about breaking with the culture of sin. Think about it. One who does not indulge in vices such as tobacco and alcohol is outside the culture of decadent indulgence. Not a part of this world. One who does not attend dances or go dating is outside the culture of promiscuity. One who does not watch the entertainments of this world has a fence in place to protect him from immorality that pollutes the mind and erodes moral values.

When Christians engage in these things, there ceases to be much difference at all between us and the world. One thing leads to another; one sin leads to another; and very quickly we experience assimilation and the collapse of moral values. The Christian finds himself crossing lines he never dreamed possible that he might cross, and soon there is no difference between the sons of the kingdom and the sons of the devil.

That is not to say that a Christian cannot enjoy alcohol, smoke a cigarette, go out on a date, attend a dance, or see a movie. But if we do not see a real and marked difference between our lives, behaviors, and moral choices and those of non-believers, we may be sure that we are not living in repentance.

PAUL GETS LEGALISTIC

The apostles also understood this. They understood that true repentance calls for a complete break with sin and the culture of sin. In their day, the culture of sin—Roman culture—was all around them. In Galatians 5, Paul makes a list of things that are off the list for Christians. He censures the Roman-era culture of his day, teaching that one who repents must repent from "the desires of the flesh," that is, physical desires:

> Now the works of the flesh are evident: sexual immorality, impurity, sensuality, idolatry, sorcery, enmity, strife, jealousy, fits of anger, rivalries, dissensions, divisions, envy, drunkenness, orgies, and things like these. I warn you, as I warned you before, that those who do such things will not inherit the kingdom of God. (Galatians 5:19–21)

Will not inherit the kingdom of God? Slow down there, Paul! That does not sound like the gospel-of-grace, justified-by-faith, not-by-works, there-is-no-condemnation-for-those-who-believe Apostle Paul whom we all know and love, does it? That sounds more like—Jesus. Jesus was always saying stuff like that: "I tell you, unless your righteousness exceeds that of the scribes and Pharisees, you will never enter the kingdom of heaven" (Matthew 5:20). It turns out that "stuff like that" constituted the first foundational, basic teaching of the Messiah. Jesus called on people to repent. Paul says, “I warn you, as I warned you before, that those who do such things will not inherit the kingdom of God.”

Once again, in Ephesians 5, Paul demonstrates his understanding of repentance from dead works:

> Sexual immorality and all impurity or covetousness must not even be named among you, as is proper among saints. Let there be no filthiness nor foolish talk nor crude joking, which are out of place, but instead let there be thanksgiving. For you may be sure of this, that everyone who is sexually immoral or impure, or who is covetous (that is, an idolater), has no inheritance in the kingdom of Christ and God. Let no one deceive you with empty words, for because of these things the wrath of God comes upon the sons of disobedience. Therefore do not become partners with them; for at one time you were darkness, but now you are light in the Lord. Walk as children of light (for the fruit of light is found in all that is good and right and true), and try to discern what is pleasing to the Lord. (Ephesians 5:3–10)

Once again, we might ask, “What happened to grace?” Paul says that a person doing these things “has no inheritance in the kingdom of Christ and God. Let no one deceive you with empty words.” A gospel message that does not demand repentance like this amounts to little more than empty words. This is not a question of earning our salvation, it is a question of repenting.

THE CHRISTIAN WHO DOES NOT REPENT

One who claims to be a Christian but persists in these sins deceives himself. He is not repenting. He is not acting as a true Christian. The Apostle John puts it this way:

> No one who abides in him keeps on sinning; no one who keeps on sinning has either seen him or known him. Little children, let no one deceive you. Whoever practices righteousness is righteous, as he is righteous. Whoever makes a practice of sinning is of the devil, for the devil has been sinning from the beginning. The reason the Son

> of God appeared was to destroy the works of the devil. No one born of God makes a practice of sinning, for God's seed abides in him, and he cannot keep on sinning because he has been born of God. By this it is evident who are the children of God, and who are the children of the devil: whoever does not practice righteousness is not of God, nor is the one who does not love his brother. (1 John 3:6–10)

Sounds like more legalism. According to these words from John, whoever practices righteousness is righteous, as Messiah is righteous.

The apostles do not imply that believers never sin. Of course we sin: "If we say we have no sin, we deceive ourselves, and the truth is not in us" (1 John 1:8). We stumble, we trip, we succumb to temptation, and sometimes we even deliberately, belligerently, willfully sin. When we do, however, we sincerely repent, confess the misdeed, renounce it, and turn away from it. No one who abides in Jesus keeps on sinning. Anyone who does has not seen him or known him.

A TOUGH SELL

Repentance from dead works is a simple concept. The gospel message begins with this imperative: quit sinning, turn around, start doing good, surrender your life and your will and everything that you are to God. Repentance is so basic and foundational that the writer of the book of Hebrews compares it to milk, the first food that a baby ingests. In other words, the Christian life begins with repentance.

Repentance does not make for a popular message in evangelicalism or in America today. A repentance-based gospel is not easy to sell. It's not a come-one, come-all, "just as I am," kind of evangelism. This is a count-the-cost message. Have you ever noticed that when people approached Jesus and asked to become his disciples, he almost inevitably put them off?

> As they were going along the road, someone said to him, "I will follow you wherever you go." And Jesus said to him,

> "Foxes have holes, and birds of the air have nests, but the Son of Man has nowhere to lay his head." To another he said, "Follow me." But he said, "Lord, let me first go and bury my father." And Jesus said to him, "Leave the dead to bury their own dead. But as for you, go and proclaim the kingdom of God." Yet another said, "I will follow you, Lord, but let me first say farewell to those at my home." Jesus said to him, "No one who puts his hand to the plow and looks back is fit for the kingdom of God." (Luke 9:57–62)

We prefer to teach a gospel that says, "Come as you are! God will bless you, and you will have a happy life." Jesus taught, "Pick up your cross and follow me." He continually taught repentance. That was his main message. He said, "Repent." Why? Because the kingdom of heaven is at hand, and when you repent, you help bring the final redemption. He said, "Repent." Why? Because the road is straight and narrow, and the gate is small that leads to life, and only a few find it.

When we take off the lenses of theological dogma and look at the Scriptures with fresh eyes, repentance is on nearly every page of the Bible. The response to the gospel message that Jesus and the apostles demanded was not merely belief or confession of belief; they called for a complete revolution of the heart, a complete renunciation of the old life of sin, sensuality, self-indulgence, selfishness, and the acts of the flesh.

When we repent in the name of Jesus of Nazareth and believe in him and in his death and resurrection as evidence of the Messiah and the Messianic Era for the forgiveness of sins, then we are born again, so to speak, and he receives us into his heart. He receives us into his family, his people, his school of disciples, his relationship with his Father, and ultimately, into his kingdom: the kingdom of heaven and the World to Come. We do not receive him into our life as much as he receives us because we surrender ourselves to him.

CHANGE YOUR MIND

Why don't preachers preach a gospel of repentance in the church today?

The grace-preaching pastor explains, "In the New Testament, repentance means 'to change your mind.' Jesus called us to change our minds by believing the good news."

He explains that we need to change our minds about Jesus and start believing that he died for our sins. He goes on to say, "If you believe that repentance means renouncing sin and turning away from disobedience, you are not living under grace, you are living under works. You are trying to live according to the Old Testament rules. In the New Testament, we do not need to deal with our sins because Jesus has already done that. Our only job is to change our mind, believe the good news, and say 'Thank you, Jesus!'"

Jesus did not speak New Testament Greek. He spoke Old Testament Aramaic and Hebrew, and the Hebrew word for "repentance" does not mean to change one's mind. It means to "turn around," that is, to change our behavior.

Are you beginning to see what I mean when I say that in much of the church today, even the basic teachings of the Messiah, the most basic elementary principles of Messiah, are no longer taught or understood? Christian anti-Law theology, especially when mixed with Protestant Reformed theology, has so twisted the Scriptures into a theological pretzel that to many pastors and teachers, almost every passage of the Bible actually means the opposite of what it seems to say.

Am I beating a dead horse here? Let's just make sure it's dead. I want you to understand exactly what I am talking about:

1. The gospel message calls on us to repent.
2. Repentance means turning away from sin.
3. The Bible defines sin as violation of the commandments of God as found in the Bible.

This is an unpopular message, because we are not going to get very far very fast with it. We are probably not going to fill stadium-sized churches with this message of repentance.

AN ONGOING DISCIPLINE

Repentance is not a one-time-only event. It requires an ongoing discipline of constantly denying the flesh, turning away from sin, saying no to the world and its temptations, turning to the LORD, and following Jesus. This is what it means to repent.

Repentance does not mean just confessing our sins and asking for forgiveness every so often. Confessing one's sins and asking for forgiveness for those sins is just the first step of repentance. Repentance means surrendering our whole life to God—our whole life: all our passions, all our desires, all our behaviors, all our motivations, all our plans, all our relationships. Repentance has something to say about how we spend our money, about what kind of house we live in, about the car we drive, about our entertainment choices, about the friendships we have, about our love life, and about our relationship with our family, our neighbors, and our colleagues at work. Repentance means actively, daily, putting the flesh (physical desires) to death by surrendering to the lordship of Jesus. It means every day, constantly working on ourselves and making war against sin in our life—rooting it out.

This is an ongoing process. The believer has to die to himself, so to speak, and live for Messiah:

> Present your bodies as a living sacrifice, holy and acceptable to God, which is your spiritual worship. Do not be conformed to this world, but be transformed by the renewal of your mind, that by testing you may discern what is the will of God, what is good and acceptable and perfect. (Romans 12:1–2)

The famous Rabbi Levi Yitzchak of Berditchev used to repent every night before saying his evening prayers. Every evening, the rabbi of Berditchev examined his heart, what he had done on that day, and repented over every flaw he discovered. For each sin that he discovered, he said, "Levi Yitzchak will not do this again." Then he chided himself, "Levi Yitzchak said exactly the same thing yesterday!" And he added, "Ah, but yesterday, Levi Yitzchak did not speak the truth. Today, he does speak the truth."

Repentance does not mean we need to be perfect. No one's perfect, but we must not be complacent in our struggle with the evil inclination.

TOAST IN THE TOASTER

The gospel of repentance implies that we need to share the gospel not just with the lost but also with the found. Most people who identify themselves as Christians do not know the authentic gospel. Most have never heard the message of repentance; they have no idea what the kingdom is, and they have no concept of the good news that our Master brought and that his apostles taught. So Christianity itself, in my opinion, is a mission field with fields white to harvest. Pray that the Lord of the harvest sends workers.

We also need to reach out with this message of universal hope and transformation to the unchurched, the lost, the secular, and the irreligious. I am a missionary at heart, and I want to share the gospel with the whole world, for God so loved the world that he sent his only Son. I am a big believer in evangelism, missions, local missions, overseas missions, missionary efforts in foreign countries, and so forth. But how do we successfully transmit a gospel of repentance?

Frankly, it's a lot of work, and I'm doing that work right now. I'm evangelizing you right now. You might think, "Now wait a minute, I am a Christian already. I made a decision to follow Jesus in 1976." That's the evangelical gospel speaking. The Messianic Jewish gospel is ongoing. It does not consist of a one-time decision. It's called discipleship, and we are never done.

People are not toast, and the gospel message is not a toaster. We put a piece of bread in a toaster, and when the toast is done, it pops up, finished and ready to eat. The evangelical gospel looks at evangelism and conversion that way. We put the bread in the toaster, turn up the heat, that is, start preaching the gospel, and when people get it, pop, they're done. They're done, and we are ready to toast some more bread.

That's not what Jesus taught us. Remember the Great Commission that he gave his disciples: "Go therefore and make disciples of all nations, baptizing them in the name of the Father and of the Son and of the Holy Spirit, teaching them to observe all that I have commanded you" (Matthew 28:19–20).

Making disciples and teaching them to observe all that Jesus commanded us does not sound like making toast in the toaster.

It sounds like serious investment into the lives of our fellow human beings.

THE MAGICAL KEY

Today one hears endless sermons about how Jesus saves, but one rarely hears the good news that the kingdom of heaven is open for everyone who willingly repents, forsakes the world, and follows Jesus. The good news is really good news, because repentance and forgiveness open the way to the kingdom, defeat the devil, and give us true freedom.

Many believers have never even honestly taken this first step. We have embraced a false gospel that taught us what to believe but did not teach us what to do. In fact, it discouraged us from doing anything more than believing. This is a gospel stripped of its power to change lives. It has produced a lukewarm religious culture that is neither hot nor cold.

Many of us have never really repented. We just believed and received. Many of us did repent, but that was long ago, and we have forgotten our first love. We have allowed the world and its vices to lull us into complacency, and in some cases, to seduce us with its temptations.

Repentance must be restored as the first foundational teaching of the Messiah. It's the first part of the message of the good news, and therefore it should be our first response to the gospel. Like a magical key, repentance opens the door to continuous obedience and submission to the Master. What credit is it to me if I have repented in the past but am living in sin today?

EVANGELIZING CHRISTIANS

The Great Commission tells us to go to all nations and raise up disciples for Jesus and to teach them everything that he taught. The gospel taught by the apostles calls for discipleship, learning, studying, continually correcting our lives, continually letting the teaching of Jesus correct us, redirect us, and transform us. It's not a one-time decision. Instead, it is a lifetime of bearing spiritual fruit by abiding in the vine and bringing forth a crop, some one hundredfold, some sixtyfold, some thirtyfold (John 15:4–5; Mark 4:8). And not a crop of souls either, but we are to bring forth a crop of repentance, good deeds, and service for the kingdom.

The problem with a one-time decision is that we can change our mind again. For example, when I get up in the morning, I always feel pretty good, and I decide, "Starting today, I'm going to eat healthier and exercise too." By the time six in the evening rolls around, my resolutions have dissolved. What happened? I made a decision. Then I made another one.

The devil does not care what you decided in 1976. He is interested in the decisions you will make today. He does not care that you prayed a prayer to receive Jesus into your heart. If you are not living for Jesus today, he has you where he wants you.

Entering the kingdom calls for an ongoing life of relationship and repentance, trust and obedience, faith and deeds, grace and law, walking in the paths of discipleship as we all strive to enter through the narrow gate, setting our eyes on Jesus, the author and perfector of our faith, seeking first the kingdom of his Father and his righteousness.

PURE JOY

Our Master had one main message that he preached everywhere he went: Quit sinning. Repent. He called this message the good news, the gospel. You might think, *Repent from sin? That does not sound like good news. That sounds like a drag.*

The flesh and the evil inclination do find repentance to be a drag. The godly soul within you (your true inner being) delights in repentance and finds pure and abundant joy in it. Sin saps life from your body and soul, but repentance is like a shot of new health. Joy comes rushing in. Repentance completes the circuit with God because in Jesus' name, repentance brings the forgiveness of sin. A person is born again, so to speak, every time he repents.

The Apostle John says, "If anyone does sin, we have an advocate with the father, Jesus Christ the righteous" (1 John 2:1). This was the cry of the penitent thief crucified with our Master to whom Jesus said, "Truly, I say to you, today you will be with me in Paradise" (Luke 23:43). If we have sinned, we should immediately repent for the wrong we have committed and strive to serve the LORD more diligently than before.

The path of repentance leads to joy. "I tell you, there will be more joy in heaven over one sinner who repents than over ninety-nine righteous persons who need no repentance" (Luke 15:7). The rabbis said, "Better is one hour of repentance and good deeds in this world than the whole life of the world to come." In his book *Love and the Messianic Age,* Messianic Jewish pioneer Paul Levertoff says, "The sinner, in whose soul the light of the divine fire has been quenched, is greater, when he repents, than the righteous who have no need for repentance." The place of the penitent sinner is even greater than that of the righteous person who does not need to repent, because the sinner throws himself entirely into the arms of God.

> In the place where penitents stand even the wholly righteous cannot stand, as it says [in Isaiah 57:19], "Peace, peace to the far and to the near." To him that was far first, and then to him that is near. (Talmud)

THE MAN WITHOUT WEDDING CLOTHES

Remember the parable about the man at the wedding banquet without wedding clothes? The banquet symbolizes the kingdom. But what do the wedding clothes represent? The book of Revelation answers this question:

> "Let us rejoice and exult and give him the glory, for the marriage of the Lamb has come, and his Bride has made herself ready; it was granted her to clothe herself with fine linen, bright and pure"—for the fine linen is the righteous deeds of the saints. And the angel said to me, "Write this: Blessed are those who are invited to the marriage supper of the Lamb." (Revelation 19:7–9)

The man without the wedding clothes symbolizes the man who thinks he will be part of the kingdom without repenting. He will not. The Apostle Paul says, "God's firm foundation stands, bearing this seal: 'The Lord knows those who are his,' and, 'Let everyone who names the name of the Lord depart from iniquity'" (2 Timothy 2:19).

And that explains why we must communicate the message of repentance along with the message of salvation. It's not enough to teach people to confess and believe—we must teach them to repent.

If you are in need of repentance, do not hesitate. Confess your sin in the name of Jesus of Nazareth and renounce it. Like the rabbi of Berditchev, declare, "Levi Yitzchak will not do that again." Start over. This very day can be the day you begin again, are born again, again, so to speak. Resolve to turn from sin. Renounce it, confess it, and surrender control of your life to Jesus. Then prepare for joy, because, after all, this is good news.

4
FAITH TOWARD GOD

> Let us leave the elementary doctrine of Christ and go on to maturity, not laying again a foundation of repentance from dead works and of faith toward God. (Hebrews 6:1)

In the late nineteenth century, Nietzsche said, "God is dead." That's nonsense, but what Nietzsche meant was that in the modern era in which he lived, faith in God was quickly dying. If that was true in his day, how much more true is it in today's postmodern era? Take a look around. The generation in which my children are consigned to live out their lives champions a self-righteous, postmodern, secular, atheist worldview. The new generation looks on people with traditional Jewish and Christian convictions with condescension if not disdain.

Despite all that, a poll of Americans taken in 2011 found that more than nine in ten Americans still believe in God. I believe that, of those nine, most have nothing resembling a clear idea about what they mean by "believing in God." When they do want God's intervention in their lives, they might offer some prayers: "God help me with this," "Help me with that." When they are frightened by circumstances beyond their control, they call on God as if he were an ace up the sleeve, but they can offer only a wishful type of prayer that is hardly different than what people call the power of positive thinking. The God to whom they pray is not necessarily the God of the Bible—the God of Abraham, Isaac, and Jacob. To them he is not a God who makes particular demands on their lives, nor does he call people to repent or condemn sin. He does not punish sin or reward righteousness.

While most people readily claim to believe in God, they are far more reluctant to acknowledge Jesus. What is it about believing in Jesus that the modern person finds so repugnant? It's not Jesus himself. Most people like the stereotypical Jesus with his long hair, his anti-establishment attitude, his peace-and-love ethic, and his smiles for children. What they do not like is the type of faith in God that Jesus represents. The writer of the book of Hebrews refers to that type of faith as one of the elementary doctrines of Christ.

HOW IS THAT DIFFERENT?

The book of Hebrews lists faith toward God as the second elementary doctrine of Christ. Why is this on the list at all? I realize that we are talking about basics, just milk, but this one seems to go without saying. The writer of the book of Hebrews was not writing to a postmodern, secular, atheist culture. He was writing to first-century Jews.

If the list of six elementary teachings were supposed to in some way characterize the uniqueness of the Messianic sect of Judaism that we call Christianity, I would expect it to exclude any basic presuppositions that the first-century Messianic Jewish believers shared in common with all the rest of the Jewish people. How does faith toward God function as a distinctive, unique hallmark of first-century Messianic Judaism? All sects of Judaism believed in God. The Pharisees, the Hillelites, the Shammaites, the Sadducees, the Boethusians, the Essenes, the Zealots, the Immersers, the what have yous—all of them believed in God, and all of them taught the concept of faith in God.

Think about it this way. Suppose you were a Baptist, and a Lutheran friend of yours said to you, "Tell me about your church. What are the fundamental things that you believe?"

If you responded, "Well, we believe in God and in the Bible and in Jesus," you have not told your friend anything. Your friend might respond, "Well, that's exactly what we believe. You must be Lutheran."

So, I don't see how this works. If we understand faith toward God to mean faith in God in the conventional sense of believing in God, that is, as an existential statement, or if it means that we pray to him and trust him for blessing, answers to prayers, and guidance in life, then how can this be a foundational principle that defines the Messianic sect of Judaism or separates it from the background of the rest of Judaism?

Imagine a conversation between a first-century Messianic Jew and his Sadducee neighbor. The Sadducee says to the Messianic Jew, "Tell me about Messianic Judaism. What are the fundamental things that you Nazarenes believe?" The Messianic Jew responds, "Well, for one thing, we believe in God." The Sadducee says, "So do we! You must be a Sadducee!"

In reality, the Sadducees did not believe in the existence of the soul, out-of-body spirits, an afterlife, the resurrection, or the final judgment. The Pharisees, on the other hand, affirmed all those things. In fact, the list of six elementary doctrines of Messiah sounds to me like a description of the foundations of Pharisaic theology. The Pharisees taught repentance; they practiced immersion and the laying on of hands; they believed in the resurrection of the dead and eternal judgment. Those were their fundamentals. So in that regard, the six foundational teachings of Messiah are not different from the six foundations of the Pharisees and not very different from other sects of Judaism—except for those of the Sadducees. The Sadducees did not teach the laying on of hands, the resurrection of the dead, or the eternal judgment, but even the Sadducees believed in God. Every religious sect of Judaism believed in God.

BELIEVE IN GOD

How can faith in God be construed to be a fundamental, distinctive teaching of the believers? The rabbis considered belief in God to be the first of the ten commandments. Maimonides, the codifier of Jewish law, lists it as positive commandment number one: "Believe in God." He lists the second commandment as "Believe God is One." This was universal across all forms of Judaism. Even the Sadducees believed this. James says, "You believe that God is one; you do well. Even the demons believe—and shudder!" (James 2:19).

Nowadays it's perfectly normal to find whole churches and synagogues in which people do not really believe that God exists. They continue to go through the religious motions just for the sake of maintaining an institutional norm. The writer of the book of Hebrews did not have our type of modern, secularized religious experience in mind. Instead, in some way, this concept of faith toward God must have set the believers apart from other sects of Judaism.

I believe that these six foundational things are categorical in nature. That means that they are broad titles for the specific teachings of Jesus and the apostles on those subjects. For example, in the previous chapter, we learned repentance from dead works, which is something the Pharisees also taught. Our apostles, however, taught it with a slightly different twist than the rest of the Pharisees did. Our apostles taught repentance in the name of the Messiah for the forgiveness of sins.

Likewise, everyone believes in God, but our apostles taught a specific type of faith toward God that they did not have in common with other sects of first-century Judaism, especially not with the reprehensible Sadducees.

FAITH ON GOD

The Greek does not say "faith in God." It says *pisteos epi Theon* (πίστεως ἐπὶ θεόν), which is better translated as "faith on God." That's not an important point, but it indicates something more than just believing in God's existence as do the shuddering demons of James 2:19. "Believe upon God" essentially communicates relying on him for something.

The writer of the book of Hebrews spends quite a bit of time developing his theology of faith upon God in Hebrews 11, where he states, "Faith is the assurance of things hoped for, the conviction of things not seen" (Hebrews 11:1). He spends a whole chapter giving us examples of men and women who lived according to faith, trusting in the promises of God even though they did not see those promises fulfilled in their lifetimes: "All these, though commended through their faith, did not receive what was promised" (Hebrews 11:39). Therefore, faith on God implies confidence that God will keep the promises he has made, despite our lack of evidence—namely, his promises about the coming of the Messiah, the final redemption, the resurrection of the dead, the kingdom of heaven, and the World to Come.

The author goes one step further and says, "Without faith it is impossible to please him, for whoever would draw near to God must believe that he exists and that he rewards those who seek him" (Hebrews 11:6). Faith is not merely believing that God exists. The author defines faith as belief that God exists and that God rewards those who seek him—in other words, the belief that God rewards merit and punishes sin. The Bible refers to this concept as the fear of the LORD.

> The fear of the LORD = belief that God rewards merit and punishes sin

In summary then, faith on God is the confident belief that God exists, he rewards merit and punishes sin, and he will make good on all the prophetic promises he has made regarding the redemption, the kingdom, and the Messiah.

BEYOND MERE HOPE

Pharisaic theology is based on the idea that God punishes sin and rewards righteousness, if not in this world, then in the afterlife and in the resurrection. The Pharisees believed that God would keep his promises. He would bring the Messiah. He was reliable, even when the evidence was not yet seen.

The Pharisees believed these things, and the disciples of Jesus believed these things. Was there anything about the way that the disciples of our Master taught "faith on God" that was different from the way the Pharisees taught it? Yes. The disciples of our Master taught faith on God on the basis of the revelation and resurrection of Jesus.

Whereas the Pharisees trusted God to fulfill his promises someday in the future, the believers had already begun to witness the fulfillment of those promises in the revelation and resurrection of Jesus.

All the great men of the Bible, from Abel, Noah, Abraham, Isaac, and Jacob up through all the judges, kings, and prophets, died in faith without seeing their faith rewarded in this world, because they did not see the fulfillment of God's promises. The generation that saw the resurrection of our Master, however, did see the first fruit of the promises fulfilled. They received the Messiah, and they saw the evidence:

> All these, though commended through their faith, did not receive what was promised, since God had provided something better for us, that apart from us they should not be made perfect. (Hebrews 11:39–40)

This is what we are talking about when we speak about believing in Jesus. In the apostolic world, the revelation, death, and resurrection of the Messiah brought faith in God to a whole new level. It went beyond faith that God exists, which all Jews believed. It even went beyond faith that God is one, which even the Sadducees believed. It went beyond faith that God will bring the kingdom and keep his promises, which even the Essenes believed. It even went beyond faith that God rewards and punishes in this world and in the next, which even the Pharisees believed. The apostles had faith in all these things on the basis that God had provided direct evidence and the beginning of its fulfillment through the revelation of Jesus of Nazareth as the Messiah and the evidence of his resurrection from the dead. That is what we mean when we talk about believing in Jesus.

BELIEVING IN JESUS

The evangelical gospel seeks to bring people to believe in Jesus. The whole objective is to believe in Jesus so that we will go to heaven. What does it mean to believe in Jesus?

To the apostles, to believe in Jesus meant to believe that he is the promised Messiah who died to bear the punishment of sin and who rose as the first fruits of the coming resurrection and a first fruits of redemption, providing a sure token of the coming kingdom of heaven on earth. It meant solid faith on God who had done this thing. The apostles taught that if God had kept his promises and had revealed his Messiah, surely he was reliable to deliver the rest of the promises. He may be relied upon to reward all those who seek him in the name of Jesus of Nazareth. To the apostles, to believe in Jesus meant to have a new, inspired, and certain faith on God.

This type of belief in Jesus presents a bigger gospel that revolves around the resurrection of Jesus. The Christian presentation of the gospel ordinarily emphasizes the significance of the death of Jesus, but the Messianic Jewish good news is equally enthralled with the resurrection of Jesus. His resurrection provides evidence of an afterlife, reward and punishment, the coming resurrection, the final redemption, the restoration of Israel, and the kingdom on earth.

This was not a different faith from that of the Pharisees. The followers of Jesus believed in all the same things in which the Pharisees believed, but they had a far more solid basis for their hope. They knew the name of the Messiah through whom God was keeping his promises. That name unleashed the power of heaven, and they no longer merely had faith in God, they experienced God.

FAITH IN GOD THROUGH JESUS

After their experiences with Jesus of Nazareth, and particularly after his resurrection, the disciples of Jesus could never again speak of faith in God or faith in the promises of God apart from their belief in Jesus, because Jesus of Nazareth had ignited their faith and made it more real and more substantial than they could have experienced apart from him. They were no longer merely practicing a religion; their religion had become their reality.

Thereafter, they could only express their relationship with God through their belief in Jesus and their relationship with him. The next time you read the New Testament Epistles, pay attention to how the apostles interweave every mention of God with a mention of Jesus. For example, Paul opens his Epistle to the Romans, "Grace to you and peace from God our Father and the Lord Jesus Christ. First, I thank my God through Jesus Christ for all of you, because your faith is proclaimed in all the world" (Romans 1:7–8). In all their writings, the apostles spoke of God through Jesus and of the gift of God in Jesus and of the grace of God given in Jesus and of the love of God in Christ Jesus. They gave praise to the God and Father of our Lord Jesus Christ, and they ascribed glory to God through Jesus Christ.

The apostles could no longer speak about God apart from their experience of Jesus of Nazareth. He had transformed their faith in God, and he had given them a different quality of faith in God.

JESUS' TEACHINGS ON FAITH

Our Master often discoursed on the subject of faith in God. He challenged his disciples to live as if they actually believed what they said they believed. In other words, he expected them to behave as if God is real and cares for us. He said to them, in essence, "Have faith in God. If you have even a mustard seed of faith in God, you will be able to move a mountain-sized problem" (Matthew 17:20). He said, "Do not worry about material things such as what you will eat and drink or about what you will wear" (Matthew 6:31). He said, "Look at the birds; look at the flowers. God takes care of them, so will he not much more take care of you, O you of little faith?" (Matthew 6:26–30). He said, "Do not worry about tomorrow, each day has enough trouble of its own" (Matthew 6:34). He sent his apostles out on missions without money or even a spare change of clothing, telling them to simply rely on God (Matthew 10:9–10). He taught them to take faith in God seriously.

Then he transformed their faith by his death and resurrection, so much so that the apostles spoke of their sect of Judaism as "the faith" and referred to each other as "believers." They believed that this powerful faith on God through the good news of the Messiah was the key to salvation, to the kingdom, and to the World to Come.

FROM FAITH FOR FAITH

According to the apostles, the gospel reveals the righteousness of God "from faith for faith." Paul says, "For in [the gospel] the righteousness of God is revealed from faith for faith, as it is written, 'The righteous shall live by faith'" (Romans 1:17). The gospel transforms mere belief into a saving faith that brings us into the kingdom and the World to Come. The prophet Habakkuk said, "The righteous shall live by his faith" (Habakkuk 2:4). The apostles understood that to mean that the righteous will obtain the resurrection and life in the World to Come by their faith. They taught that this transformed, Messianic faith justifies even sinners. The Apostle Peter taught that God cleansed the hearts of both Jewish and Gentile believers by this same faith. Paul wrote, "Since we have been justified by faith, we have peace with God through our Lord Jesus Christ. Through him we have also obtained access by faith into this grace in which we stand, and we rejoice in hope of the glory of God" (Romans 5:1–2).

JUDAISM AND MESSIANIC JUDAISM

Faith on God through Jesus of Nazareth is the only substantial difference between traditional Judaism and Messianic Judaism. The Pharisees, the fathers of modern Judaism, believed all the same things that the apostles did, but they did not have the benefit of the revelation of Jesus and the evidence of his resurrection. The Pharisees believed all the same things that the disciples did, but the disciples had personally experienced those things through their contact with Jesus of Nazareth. That contact forever linked their faith toward God with the good news of the story and teachings of Jesus.

I was once having a conversation with an anxious young Christian. He was troubled at coming to the realization that the Jewish people also have a genuine faith in God and in the coming of Messiah and so forth. This realization bothered him because suddenly he felt as if his own faith was no longer unique or special. He asked me, "What's the difference between us and them? Why is it so important to believe in Jesus?"

Despite my best efforts, I don't think that question was ever resolved for him, because today he is no longer a disciple. He converted to Judaism and denied his faith in Jesus.

It is true that we do believe the same things about the same God and read the same Scriptures as those Jews who do not believe in Jesus as the Messiah. In Messianic Judaism, we are even part of the same religion. Despite all that common ground, there is one great difference between us. The difference is not in *what* we believe about God but in *how* we believe about God.

Devout Jewish people who do not believe in Jesus as the Messiah believe the same things about God that we believe, but they do not do so in light of the revelation, teaching, death, and resurrection of Jesus. They believe outside the light of that transforming, from-faith-for-faith experience that Paul spoke of when he said, "I am not ashamed of the gospel, for it is the power of God for salvation to everyone who believes, to the Jew first and also to the Greek" (Romans 1:16).

THE TWO DAUGHTERS

Let me explain the difference by way of a parable.

Once, a man who had two daughters went off to war. Before he left, he promised to return to them, and he also promised them, "When I return, I will bring you each a fine string of pearls and a summer dress." No one except the two girls knew about the promise. After many years, the man had not returned, and everyone presumed him dead. His daughters, however, continued to hope, believe, and wait. A decade passed, and they grew to become adult women, but neither of them forgot their father or his promises. Deep in their hearts, they continued to hope and to believe. One day a messenger came seeking the girls. Finding only one daughter, he told her, "I have news of your father. He is returning, and he sends you this gift." The messenger presented her with a fine string of pearls.

Now both girls still believed the promise of the father, but one had received a token of the promise, and the other had not. One had faith in the father's promise on the basis of her hope and confidence in the father's promise, but the other had faith in the father's promise on the basis of the good news that she had already received and on the basis of the partial fulfillment of her father's promise. She already held the pearls. She had no question in her mind that she would soon see her father face to face. Think of that girl's confidence, certainty, and joy. She no longer had any doubt that her father was coming. She knew that he would bring the summer dress because she had already received the pearls.

Faith on God is a fundamental teaching of Messiah. It entails confidence that God rewards and punishes, that he is just, that he keeps his word, and that he is therefore reliable. He can be trusted because of the evidence we have received through the revelation and resurrection of Jesus. We may be confident in him because of the good news we have already heard and the tokens he has already bestowed.

THE OBEDIENCE OF FAITH

The faith on God that the apostles taught is a life-changing faith that should impact us on every level. It provides the motivation for repentance from dead works. It grants everyone who believes a new lease on life—a whole new reason to live. The Master referred to this type of faith as being born again. The apostles compared it to dying and being resurrected.

This type of faith toward God has little in common with the type of belief in God espoused by nine out of ten Americans in that 2011 polling data I mentioned above. We are not speaking of vague, superstitious belief in a "god" or a spiritual force. Instead, we are talking about faith on the God of Israel and confidence in his promises in light of the Messiah and because of the Messiah. We are speaking about the God of Abraham, Isaac, and Jacob, the God of the Bible. This type of faith affirms that God is true, his Torah is true, his Word is true, and that he is utterly reliable, faithful, and trustworthy. Faith on God is that transforming faith of which Habakkuk spoke when he said, "The righteous will live by his faith" (Habakkuk 2:4).

Paul referred to Messianic faith on God as "the obedience of faith." People usually do not put those two words together, but the apostles did. They saw an absolute relationship between faith and obedience:

> [God] is able to strengthen you according to my gospel and the preaching of Jesus Christ, according to the revelation of the mystery that was kept secret for long ages but has now been disclosed and through the prophetic writings has been made known to all nations, according

> to the command of the eternal God, to bring about the obedience of faith. (Romans 16:25–26)

Here we see that God bestowed the revelation of Messiah to bring about the obedience of faith. Again, this is what the apostles meant when they talked about believing in Jesus. Faith is a lot more than "Do you believe Jesus died for your sins? You do? Good. Then you will go to heaven when you die."

Church creeds define faith in God as points of dogma that must be confirmed, but Jesus seemed far less worried about *what* we believed about God than about *how* we believed in God. Faith toward God entails obedience, relationship, trust, and a life of confidence like that of the birds of the air, which neither sow nor reap nor store away in barns, and like that of the grass of the field, which neither toils nor spins. It implies trusting in the goodness of God to make things right in the end and trusting that everything is in his hands because he ultimately rewards the good and punishes the bad.

If a person accepts all these things, he must submit himself and give himself over to this God. Faith requires repenting and renouncing sin, because this God punishes sin. It requires obedience and good works, because this God rewards righteousness. At the same time, the person with this depth of faith and confidence in the God and Father of Jesus does not rely on his own righteousness or good works to obtain standing before God, because everything about this faith toward God is conducted only through the revelation of Jesus. The Messiah who suffered on our behalf is the source of eternal salvation for all who believe.

Peter summarizes our faith toward God through the revelation of Jesus in just a few words:

> He was foreknown before the foundation of the world but was made manifest in the last times for the sake of you who through him are believers in God, who raised him from the dead and gave him glory, so that your faith and hope are in God. (1 Peter 1:20–21)

5
INSTRUCTION ABOUT WASHINGS

> Let us leave the elementary doctrine of Christ and go on to maturity, not laying again a foundation of repentance from dead works and of faith toward God, and of instruction about washings. (Hebrews 6:1–2)

I grew up in a Christian home, and as an evangelical child, I grew up immersed in a religious environment in which eternal consequences remained continually in view. When I was three or four years old, I thought through the questions of life and death one day while playing alone with a fine set of Tonka fire trucks. I thought about my poor behavior, and I said to myself, "I hope that I am good enough to get into heaven when I die." I had no sooner thought the thought than it occurred to me that my Sunday school teacher had been saying that no one is good enough to get into heaven. We must accept Jesus into our hearts to obtain that eternal reward. I decided to do so immediately, so I abandoned the Tonka trucks and sought out my mother. I asked her to help me pray, and she did, tearfully and with great sincerity. Ever since then, I have been a Christian.

When I was about thirteen years old or so, my father asked me if I would like to be baptized. In our church tradition, we delayed the baptism of children until they were old enough to voluntarily consent to the ceremony.

I replied, "No, not yet."

We had the same conversation several months later and then again after that. My father never pressed me for an explanation, but even if he had, I would not have told him the real reason for my hesitation. At that time, I still contemplated the possibility of choosing the secular path of a sinner. You might think that I did not understand baptism. On the contrary, I understood it too well. I understood that it signified a lifelong commitment to Jesus, and I did not feel certain about agreeing to a commitment of that magnitude. Around the age of fifteen, I thought the matter through more thoroughly. I realized that if God did exist, it made no logical sense to choose a path in life contrary to his will and revelation. I consented to be baptized, and I emerged from the water both wet and a disciple of Jesus, although I have rarely been a good one.

INSTRUCTION ABOUT WASHINGS

In previous chapters we have learned the foundation of repentance from dead works and the foundation of faith toward God. Repentance from dead works means turning away from sin, renouncing it, repenting, and turning to God for the forgiveness of sins in the name of Jesus. Faith toward God means a firm fear of the LORD, the belief that God punishes sin and rewards righteousness, and a firm belief in his prophetic promises, which are all made "yes, yes" in Messiah (2 Corinthians 1:20). This is faith in God through belief in Jesus as our Master taught: "Believe in God; believe also in me" (John 14:1).

In this chapter, we press on to the third foundational principle of our religion: "instruction about washings."

What does that mean? Apparently we should know. Instruction about washings is considered so basic, so fundamental to faith in Jesus, that the writer of the Epistle to the Hebrews compares it to milk; it's not even solid food. If that is the case, why do we have no idea what he is talking about?

In this chapter, we are going to do our best to discover an ancient Christian ritual practiced by the early first-century believers but long since lost and forgotten. We will be like Indiana Jones seeking a lost artifact from long ago. What is this lost artifact? Not the ark of the covenant. Not this time. This time it's something called *baptismon didachis* (βαπτισμῶν διδαχῆς), or "instruction about washings." *Baptismon* is the plural of *baptismos* (βαπτισμός), which simply means a submersion in water, usually for washing. You can hear the close relationship to the Greek word *baptisma* (βάπτισμα), which our English Bibles translate as "baptism," but it means immersion or submersion. In a Jewish context, it refers specifically to ceremonial immersion in a pool of living water for the sake of obtaining ritual purity. *Didachis* means "instruction" or "teaching."

BAPTISM

The early believers practiced baptism into the name of Jesus by immersing themselves in water for his sake and in the authority of his name. The ceremony marked a new believer's initiation into the school of Jesus' disciples. Although baptism into the name of Jesus was a one-time event that marked the beginning of a person's life of discipleship, that single immersion was not the only time a person underwent ritual immersion.

If you have studied Messianic Judaism before, you have probably already learned about baptism and its relationship to immersion in a mikvah. For those readers who have not yet had that opportunity, suffice it to say, pretty much everything you have ever been told or learned about baptism—its meaning, how it was done, what it accomplishes, why people did it, and why we should do it today—is historically inaccurate. Baptism was not practiced only by Christians. It was not a new Christian ritual. It did not remove original sin. It was not administered to infants and children. It was not a sacrament. It did not involve the sprinkling of water (except in certain circumstances). It did not involve a baptizer dunking or immersing another person into water. It was not ordinarily a public event. Moreover, Jewish people practiced (and still do practice) many types of baptism for many different reasons.

JEWISH BAPTISM

As mentioned above, the Greek word *baptisma* (βάπτισμα) means submersion. Jesus told his disciples to immerse new disciples in his name. He did not need to tell them how to conduct an immersion because they were Jewish and were already familiar with the ceremony. Submersion in water for ritual purification was a common part of Jewish life in the first century. Jewish people immersed in water to remove Levitical impurity. The Torah prohibited the ritually impure from entering the Temple and from eating of the sacrifices until they had immersed in living water. The priests immersed every day.

Immersion for purification entails a full body baptism into "living water," that is, naturally flowing water: rain, spring, or river water that has not been artificially drawn from a well or cistern. In the days of John the Immerser and the apostles, observant Jews immersed by descending into a naturally fed pool or gathering of water (a river or lake will do) and submerging themselves completely below the surface. The Hebrew word for such a natural gathering of water is *mikvah* (מקוה).

People immerse in the mikvah for other reasons as well. After a woman completes menstruation, she immerses in a mikvah before rejoining her husband—a ritual still practiced in Judaism today. Moreover, Gentiles undergoing conversion to Judaism immerse in a mikvah as their final rite of passage. A Gentile male who wants to become Jewish must undergo both circumcision and immersion. Female converts are merely immersed. The immersion symbolizes a legal change in status. The new initiate enters the water as a Gentile

A ritual bath from Temple times. Image: Wikimedia Commons (Goldberg)

but emerges from the water with a new legal identity. The disciples of Jesus used immersion for a similar induction ceremony. A person who immersed himself in the name of Jesus underwent a spiritual and legal change of status. He entered the water as a non-disciple and emerged as a disciple and follower of Jesus.

The archaeological remains of first-century Jewish settlements in the land of Israel shed light on the importance of immersion in daily Jewish life. Wherever Jews lived, they created immersion baths in the rock. Archaeologists today consider the presence of a mikvah among archaeological remains as evidence of Jewish occupation, and they have uncovered hundreds of such baths throughout the land.

ARCHAEOLOGY OF THE MIKVAH

We could go to Masada, where the Jewish revolutionaries made their last stand against Rome in the days of the apostles. Herod the Great had built the rocky plateau of Masada into a fortress and palace. The Zealots converted bathhouses and cisterns on Masada into immersion pools so that they could immerse themselves for ritual purity on a regular basis.

We could go to Qumran, where the Dead Sea Scrolls were found. The Essene Jews who lived there immersed themselves daily for ritual purity as part of their monastic lifestyle in the Judean wilderness beside the Dead Sea. They shared all things in common, living celibately and communally, and they daily dipped themselves in the mikvah.

We could go to the holy Temple Mount in Jerusalem, where all the worshipers passed through a mikvah before entering the Temple. A person going to the Temple could immerse himself in any one of dozens, even hundreds, of mikvahs before going into the Temple.

While in Jerusalem, we could visit the priests' quarters, where archaeologists have uncovered mikvahs in the basements of priestly mansions. We could visit the recently excavated pool of Siloam, which, to everyone's surprise, apparently functioned as a large public mikvah.

In fact, we could visit just about any excavation where Jewish people lived in the Apostolic Era, and I could show you these rock-cut baths that look like deep cisterns. They are usually about six feet deep or more. Stone-cut steps descend into them. These things are everywhere.

I don't think that I am exaggerating when I say that in Christianity we have completely misunderstood and misapplied baptism because we have taken it outside its Jewish context. Jesus and the apostles would probably not recognize the ceremony that we call baptism as baptism.

Don't get me wrong. I am not interested in dismantling Roman Catholic, Eastern Orthodox, Lutheran, Reformed, Presbyterian, or Anabaptist interpretations of baptism. Each branch of Christianity has developed its own unique traditions and interpretations of the concept. All the various permutations of the ceremony have a common origin in Jewish immersion rituals, but they have taken on new modes and meanings in their various faith traditions. There is nothing wrong with that, but in Messianic Judaism, we do not have the freedom to be so creative. Our objective is to reconcile our faith and practice with that of the New Testament believers. For that reason, we need to understand, teach, learn, and practice baptism as it was understood, taught, and practiced by Jesus and the apostles. We are in the business of restoring early Messianic Judaism, so we need to set aside the later developments of church tradition in order to return to the original form.

A SILLY INTERPRETATION

The English Standard Version of Hebrews 6:2 lists instruction about washings as a basic teaching of Messiah. Why does the ESV translate it in these terms? Why not translate it as the King James Version does: "the doctrine of baptisms"? Why not translate it as the New International Version does: "instruction about baptisms"? The translators of the English Standard Version, like many Bible scholars, recognized that the Greek word *baptismon* does not sound as if it's talking about Christian baptism, because it appears in the plural form, whereas Christians are baptized only once. Furthermore, in other places in the New Testament, the word *baptismos* refers to ceremonial purification rituals of immersion in a mikvah. Several scholars looked at this passage and said, "I don't think he's talking about Christian baptism. I think he's talking about Jewish purity rituals."

Some go so far as to explain that instruction about washings is instruction not to participate in Levitical purification ceremonies, since those things have all been canceled and done away with. In other words, according to this absurd interpretation, instruction about washings is the instruction that a Christian Jew should not be using a mikvah or practicing the Levitical laws any longer. In that case, one would have to understand it to mean "instruction about not participating in Jewish washings and other ceremonies."

This is similar to the interpretation that says that repentance from dead works means turning away from the ceremonial practices of Judaism. Who comes up with this stuff? I mean, if you believed that, you would have to believe that two out of six fundamental doctrines of Messiah are a renunciation of Torah, the Temple, and the Levitical system. That's not what it means.

ANOTHER SILLY INTERPRETATION

So what does it mean?

Well, if you had asked me a few years ago, I would have told you that the passage refers to instructions about how to do immersions. Not just immersions into the name of Messiah or a convert's immersion for the new Christian but different immersions for different reasons such as ritual purity and so forth. In other words, instruction about washings was a basic primer on how and when to use the mikvah, including your initial baptism in the name of Messiah. I would have explained the plural form of the word "washings" as including other ceremonial washings.

As I thought more about that interpretation, I realized that it was dead wrong. Why would Jewish believers in the first century need instructions about how and when to use a mikvah? That's ridiculous. First-century Jewish people knew what a mikvah was, how to make one, and when to use it. They did not need anyone's instructions in that. Again, the mikvah is one of the most common, telltale signs of Jewish occupation in the archaeological record. Archaeologists can always identify the remains of a Jewish community when they find the remains of a mikvah. Jewish people, like the ones to whom the Epistle to the Hebrews is directed, did not need to be instructed about how to make a mikvah or how to use one.

If "instruction about washings" means "instruction about how and when to use the mikvah," then it begs the question, "Why aren't *all* the ceremonial elements included in this list of basics?" Why does the list of elementary teachings omit "instruction about keeping Passover" or "instruction about keeping kosher" or "instruction about times of prayer" and so forth?

Clearly, instruction about washings cannot have been instruction about how, when, or why to undergo ritual immersion. It was not about ritual purity or even about how to immerse new believers into the faith. No one needed to be taught about that in the Jewish community. When Simon Peter said to the people in Acts 2, "Repent and be baptized every one of you in the name of Jesus Christ for the forgiveness of your sins" (Act 2:38), no one said, "Baptized? What is that? How do you do it?" He was speaking to Jewish people, and they all knew what it meant. Likewise, the writer of the Epistle to the Hebrews is writing to Jews. They all knew what immersion was and how it was done, and they all knew what immersion in the name of Jesus the Messiah was and how it was done because they had all been through it themselves.

CATECHETICAL INSTRUCTION

In the Word Biblical Commentary on the book of Hebrews, William Lane points out that several early Greek manuscripts used the accusative case of *didachin* (διδαχήν) rather than the genitive *didachis* (διδαχῆς), and he argues that this is the older, authentic version. It hardly makes a big difference, but on that basis, he felt confident in translating "instruction about washings" as "the Catechetical instruction concerning cleansing rites." In other words, it was the catechism a new initiate into the faith had to learn before he could receive immersion in the name of Jesus of Nazareth. This interpretation brings to mind the first-century apostolic initiation document *Didachi kurion dia ton dodika apostolon tois ethnesin*, which means *The Instruction of the Master through the Twelve Apostles to the Gentiles.* We call it, as we noted earlier, the *Didache* (Διδαχή), or *The Instruction.*

In Christianity today, a catechism is a summary of basic teachings and doctrines presented to children prior to their confirmation into the faith and presented to adults who are converting to join the church. That's exactly what the *Didache* was.

DISCOVERY OF THE DIDACHE

Sometime in the decades after the fall of Jerusalem, apostolic authorities composed the *Didache* as a simple treatise that they addressed to the ever-growing numbers of Gentile disciples. It represents a distillation of the teachings of Jesus that the twelve apostles conveyed to their Gentile disciples. The document essentially tries to communicate, in the words of Jesus, the basic path of Torah and ethical monotheism as it applies to the God-fearing Gentile believers.

The document was well-known in the early church, but it fell out of use over time and eventually disappeared. Scholars knew about it only because early church writers mentioned it, but no one had seen it for centuries. Then in 1873, as in a scene from Indiana Jones or the Sean Connery movie *Name of the Rose*, Archbishop Philotheos Bryennios, the Greek Orthodox Metropolitan of Nicomeida, was doing some research in the Jerusalem Monastery of the Most Holy Sepulcher in Constantinople. (Constantinople was once, long ago, the capital of Byzantine Christianity, named after Emperor Constantine himself. It fell to the Ottomans in the Middle Ages, and they renamed it Istanbul.) The library contained ancient documents going back to when Istanbul was still Constantinople. Bryennios opened an old codex containing several pieces of early-church literature, including the *Epistle of Barnabus*, the two epistles of *Clement*, the long form of the Ignatian Letters, and the *Didache*.[1]

At first many scholars considered the discovery a forgery. It seemed too good to be true. Imagine finding a document composed by the early first-century believers that had been missing for 1,800 years. It was not a fake. And it was full of surprises.

No one really liked it. The Roman Catholics did not like it because it did not seem to support Catholic theology. The Eastern Orthodox Church did not like it because it did not seem to support Orthodox theology. The Protestants did not like it because it did

---

1 J.B. Lightfoot, J.R. Harmer, *The Apostolic Fathers* (2nd ed.; Michael Holmes, ed.; Grand Rapids, MI: Baker Book House, 1989), 147.

not seem to support Protestant theology. They all claimed that it validated their respective theologies, but it did not.

The contents sounded so Jewish that many scholars suspected that the *Didache* might have originally been a Jewish document that had been "Christianized" by the church, but that theory has also been abandoned. Today most scholars admit that the document originated from Jewish believers who were writing a few decades after the destruction of the Second Temple in 70 CE.

A PRIMER IN ETHICAL MONOTHEISM

The first six chapters of the *Didache* consist of a primer in ethical monotheism based mainly on the teachings of Jesus and select passages of Torah. We refer to this section as "The Two Ways" because the section begins with the words, "There are two ways: one of life and one of death." The *Didache* goes on to describe the difference:

> There are two ways: one of life and one of death; however, there is a great difference between the two ways. Now the Way of Life is this: first, you shall love God who made you; second, you shall love your fellow as yourself. Whatever you do not want to happen to you, do not do to one another. This is the teaching about these matters:
>
> Speak well of those who speak ill of you, and pray for your enemies; fast for those who persecute you, for what special favor do you merit if you love those who love you? Do not even the Gentiles do the same? However, you are to love those who hate you, and you will not have any enemies.
>
> Restrain yourself from natural and physical inclinations: if someone strikes you on the right cheek, turn the other to him, and you will be complete. If someone forces you to go one mile, go with him two. If someone takes away your cloak, give him your tunic also. If someone takes away what is yours, do not demand it back, for you are not even able to get it back. (*Didache* 1:1–4, Vine of David translation)

As the excerpt above illustrates, the *Didache* distills the words and teachings of Jesus to present the basics of discipleship. It goes on with more material like this for six chapters, laying out the way of life and the way of death, declaring acts of righteousness and acts of wickedness, differentiating between wrong and right, and teaching the basics of Christian living as defined by early Jewish believers. It presents the basics of the Torah, such as the Ten Commandments, and basic ethical instruction on godly living.

INSTRUCTION CONCERNING BAPTISM

After presenting six chapters of moral instructions derived from the Torah and the teachings of Jesus, the *Didache* shifts abruptly into a short discussion on how to conduct an immersion. It says, "having first said all these things"—meaning the first six chapters of ethical and moral instruction—the candidate is ready to undergo immersion:

> Concerning immersion, immerse in this way: Having first said all these things, immerse in the name of the Father and the Son and the Holy Spirit in living water. But if you do not have living water, immerse in other water; and if you cannot immerse in cold water, then immerse in warm water. But if you do not have either [in sufficient quantity to immerse], pour water on the head three times in the name of the Father and the Son and the Holy Spirit. Prior to the immersion, the one performing the immersion and the one being immersed should fast beforehand, and also any others if they can. Require the one being immersed to fast one or two days prior to the immersion. (*Didache* 7:1–4, Vine of David translation)

This is instruction about washings, that is, catechetical instruction regarding baptisms. Based on the evidence in the *Didache*, we can deduce that the term "instruction about washings" refers to the period of instruction and the contents of that instruction that a new initiate into the school of Jesus' disciples underwent prior to immersion into Jesus' name. Before the community allowed the new initiate to receive baptism, it required him to undergo a catechetical period of instruction. The writer of the book of Hebrews must have had something very similar to the *Didache* in mind when he referred to instruction about washings. The "instruction" refers not as much to the mode of immersion as it does to the teaching that must precede immersion. Before going into the water, the new initiate needed to understand the teachings of Jesus concerning the two ways: the way of life and the way of death. The candidate needed to understand the difference between the narrow path that leads to life and the wide path that leads to destruction.

I am not suggesting that the *Didache* was the only instruction concerning baptisms or that all believers used the same written catechism. More likely, spiritual mentors conveyed the teaching orally. The *Didache* may represent an attempt to standardize the instruction. It represents only one example of the instruction, and it happens to be written for Gentile disciples. Both Jewish and Gentile believers needed to learn the catechetical instructions regarding immersions prior to their baptism.

JOINING THE SCHOOL

Immersion into the name of Jesus symbolized joining his school of disciples, joining his spiritual family, and becoming a member of the club. It assumed that the new initiate had consented to submit to Jesus' teaching and authority. Before a person could do that, he had to know something about that teaching and authority. A person needed to have a fairly good idea of what he was committing himself to before his immersion. The catechetical instructions regarding immersions prepared the potential disciple for making that choice.

The apostles did not want people randomly joining the assembly of Jesus without even knowing what that meant or what would be expected of them. They wanted people to make an informed decision.

We can see a clear progression in the elementary teaching of the Messiah: First, repent from sin. Second, place faith in God through Jesus. Then, if a person has completed the first two things, he is ready to learn the teachings of Jesus. If he agrees to consent to the teachings of Jesus and to submit himself to them, then he is ready to undergo immersion in his name and to join the fraternity (or sorority) of his disciples. That's the way they did it in the days of the apostles, and that was the milk, the basics, the elementary stuff.

This corresponds exactly with what Jesus told his disciples to do. He said, "Go therefore and make disciples of all nations, baptizing them in the name of the Father and of the Son and of the Holy Spirit, teaching them to observe all that I have commanded you" (Matthew 28:19–20). The Great Commission commands us to teach the new disciples to observe all that Jesus commanded us to do.

COUNTING THE COST

In my opinion, we need to bring this elementary stuff back. Too much of the church has already been hijacked by false converts who were baptized into it, usually (as babies) without their consent, unconverted, with unconverted hearts. Even as adults prepared for baptism, their catechism probably involved learning theological formulas and reciting certain dogmas, but it probably did not lay out a basic moral, ethical code of conduct based upon the teaching of Jesus.

The instruction about baptisms reminds me of another first-century sectarian movement by a group called the Essenes. If a person wanted to become an Essene, he could join the community, but he was kept on probation for the first year. During that year, he learned the community rules and the way of life. The Essenes had a document called "The Community Rule." New initiates probably learned this during their probationary year in the community.

The Essene community gave new initiates twelve months to decide if they wanted to commit to the monk-like Essene life. If, after living as an Essene and with the Essenes for that year, the candidate decided the rigors were too difficult, he could opt out. If, on the other hand, he decided he wanted to be an Essene, he took a lifetime vow to live as an Essene. One thing that a candidate could not do was to hang around the community indefinitely, uncommitted, with one foot in the community and one foot out.

It does not surprise me at all that the disciples of Jesus had a similar probationary period of intense instruction that culminated with immersion. It might not have been a year or any fixed amount of time, but it was surely important to the apostles that people counted the cost before committing to the high calling of discipleship to Jesus. The demands of discipleship are high. Discipleship requires taking up one's cross, dying to the self, and being ready to die for the name of Jesus—not something to be entered into casually or haphazardly.

BORN OF WATER AND THE SPIRIT

Our investigation into instruction about washings has led us from Masada to Qumran to Jerusalem to the Temple to Constantinople. We have learned that during the days of the apostles, new disciples counted the cost before committing to a life of discipleship. They learned the basic teachings of Jesus and the standards of being his disciples, and they agreed to adopt that code of conduct before they were received into the water of immersion. This might have been something that was done quickly, or it might have taken as long as a year of preparation. Each case was probably different. When the leaders of the community felt the initiate had satisfactorily completed the catechetical period of instruction, they received the new disciple into the community through the ceremony of immersion into our Master's name. Then he went down into the water, descended into a mikvah.

If the person was Jewish, it was not the first time in his life that he had immersed in a mikvah, but it was the first time that the person did so in the name of Jesus of Nazareth. When he emerged from the water, the community received the new initiate as a brother or sister in the fellowship of the disciples with joy and congratulation—not unlike the joy a family feels at the birth of a newborn child. He was received as one born again, "born of water and the Spirit" (John 3:5).

6
THE LAYING ON OF HANDS

> Let us leave the elementary doctrine of Christ and go on to maturity, not laying again a foundation of repentance from dead works and of faith toward God, and of instruction about washings, the laying on of hands. (Hebrews 6:1–2)

In the year that my daughter was born, unbeknownst to me I developed pneumonia in both lungs. I had been working in apartment maintenance, and I had picked up a job clearing up black-mold infestations in apartments in which the nefarious stuff had overrun whole walls. I concocted a remedy for the infestations by combining various vapor sealers and then painting over the mold with fungicide-laced paint. I wore a respirator, but despite the precaution, I apparently had breathed the spores into my lungs where they began to cause trouble. Soon I developed a nasty case of walking pneumonia, but I did not realize it. I only knew that I had a terrible, persistent cough and shortness of breath. It started ominously on the eve of Yom Kippur. By Sukkot it had escalated to the point at which I could barely teach, but I had to keep teaching: cough, cough, teach, teach, teach, cough, cough, teach, teach, and so forth.

After a few weeks of this, two women from a Messianic congregation approached me at the conclusion of a Torah study I had led. They said, "You sound terrible, and this has been going on for several weeks. Would you mind if we prayed for you?"

I replied, "I would not mind at all; just please don't lay hands on me."

That was probably rude, but it seemed to me an innocent, reasonable request. I do not want women to whom I am not married touching me in any case, much less women I hardly know exercising their dubious spiritual powers on my behalf. They consented to my terms and prayed over me without laying hands on me, for which I was grateful, but I later heard that I had deeply offended both of them. Apparently, I had committed a serious *faux pas* in charismatic Christian culture.

In the end, it all came out right. I apologized to them, went to the doctor, and received antibiotics that—with God's help—eventually cleared my lungs. From then on, however, I had a reputation in the local Messianic community as a quencher of the Holy Spirit.

LAYING ON OF HANDS

What is this ritual of "laying on of hands" all about?

In the days of the apostles, believers took certain doctrines for granted as obvious, elementary, baby stuff: the elementary teachings of the Messiah. The Epistle to the Hebrews lists the laying on of hands as one of those elementary teachings.

In previous chapters, we learned that the foundation of repentance from dead works calls for turning away from sin, renouncing sin, and submitting our wills and our lives to God.

Faith toward God implies exercising the fear of the LORD and confidence in God based upon the revelation and resurrection of the Messiah. Instruction about washings means the catechetical instruction that a new believer receives prior to his immersion.

Those first three foundational teachings present a sort of basic progression for the new believer. He hears the gospel message, "Repent, for the kingdom of heaven is at hand," and he repents from dead works. He places his faith in God through the revelation of the Messiah. He receives some basic instruction in the teachings of Jesus before undergoing immersion into living water in the name of the Master. And then—the laying on of hands.

Three different functions for the ceremonial laying on of hands appear in the Bible: bestowing blessings, ritual substitution, and ordination into office. Many New Testament readers will be quick to add to the list impartation of divine healing, but healing belongs to the broader category of bestowing a blessing. A prayer for healing functions as a form of blessing. Which of these types of laying on of hands did the writer of the book of Hebrews have in mind when he listed the ritual among the elementary teachings of Messiah?

1. Bestowing blessings
    a. Upon children
    b. Upon disciples
    c. Upon petitioners
    d. Upon the sick
2. Ritual substitution
    a. Sacrificial animals
    b. Levites
3. Ordination
    a. Moses to Joshua
    b. Elders and rabbis
    c. Conferring the Spirit

BESTOWING BLESSINGS AND HEALING

When the patriarchs blessed their sons, they laid hands on their heads. Remember, when Jacob blessed Joseph's sons Ephraim and Mannaseh, he crossed his arms to lay his right hand on the head of Ephraim and his left hand on the head of Mannaseh (Genesis 48:14). On the basis of that story, fathers lay hands on their children when bestowing blessings upon them at the Friday night Sabbath table. Rebbes and holy men bless their disciples and petitioners who come seeking prayer. In the Gospels, Jesus blessed children by laying his hands on them:

> And they were bringing children to Jesus that he might touch them ... and he took them in his arms and blessed them, laying his hands on them." (Mark 10:13, 16)

> Then children were brought to him that he might lay his hands on them and pray. (Matthew 19:13)

Since Judaism associated the laying on of hands with conferring a blessing, Jewish people naturally conferred prayers for healing the same way. For example, in Mark 5, one of the rulers of the Capernaum synagogue asked Jesus to heal his daughter by laying his hands upon her: "Come and lay your hands on her, so that she may be made well and live" (Mark 5:23). (According to a legend appearing in the Dead Sea Scrolls, Abraham once healed the king of Egypt by laying his hands on Pharaoh's head. This legend indicates that the custom of healing through the laying on of hands and prayer was something practiced among Jews in general in the days of Jesus.) The laying on of hands for the sake of healing was not unique to Jesus and his followers. Jesus did not introduce a new ceremonial ritual when he laid hands on the sick.

In the long ending of the book of Mark, Jesus says that his disciples "will lay their hands on the sick, and they will recover" (Mark 16:18). In the book of Acts, Ananias of Damascus lays hands on Paul and prays for him, and he recovers his eyesight. While stranded on Malta, Paul healed a man sick with fever and dysentery: "Paul visited him and prayed, and putting his hands on him healed him" (Acts 28:8). In the congregations of believers, this duty fell to the elders, as James writes: "Is anyone among you sick? Let him call for the elders of the assembly, and let them pray over him" (James 5:14). Once again, let me remind you, Jewish people use the ceremony of laying on of hands not just for healing. They primarily use it for conferring a blessing upon someone.

Is this what Hebrews 6:2 has in mind? Is the conferring of blessings and healings one of the elementary principles of Messiah? Don't answer, because we have yet to learn about another type of laying on of hands in the Torah.

RITUAL SUBSTITUTION

Judaism uses the Hebrew word *semichah,* (סמיכה) to mean the laying on of hands. The book of Leviticus describes how a worshiper bringing a sacrifice to the Temple laid hands (*semichah*) on his animal before offering it to the LORD:

> He shall lay his hand on the head of the burnt offering, and it shall be accepted for him to make atonement for him. (Leviticus 1:4)

When a person brought a sacrifice to the Temple, he laid hands on it before offering it to the LORD. The worshiper regarded the sacrificial animal as a substitute for himself. He offered it at "the entrance of the tent of meeting, that he may be accepted before the LORD" (Leviticus 1:3). In that respect, the sacrifice represented a ritual surrogate for the person offering. The first ritual procedure required the laying on of hands (*semichah,* סמיכה). The act of *semichah* implied a physical "leaning" on the animal so that the weight of the man transferred to the animal. The ceremony took place in the courtyard of the Temple, where the animal was slain. It had to be performed with bare hands. It symbolized both ownership of the animal and an investment of the man's identity into the animal. The ritual declared, "This is my animal, and it represents me as it goes to the altar." In some cases, when appropriate to do so with a sin offering, the person offering the animal confessed sins while laying his hands on the head of a sacrifice.

The same laying-on-of-hands terminology appears in Numbers 8:10 in which all Israel laid their hands upon the Levites to designate their tribe as surrogates in the worship of the LORD on behalf of the whole nation. The Israelites laid hands upon the Levites to designate them as substitutes in their place. Then the Levites laid their hands on bulls to designate them as substitutes in their place.

Is that what the writer of the book of Hebrews has in mind? Did he have the sacrificial procedure in mind when he identified the laying on of hands as one of the elementary teachings of Jesus?

ORDINATION

Judaism also uses the ritual of laying on of hands to indicate an investment of identity and authority in an ordination ritual. Not long before Moses died, he asked the LORD to appoint a successor for him. He wanted to leave behind a man to lead Israel the way a good shepherd guides a flock. The LORD told Moses, "Take Joshua the son of Nun, a man in whom is the Spirit, and lay your hand on him" (Numbers 27:18). He explained the meaning of the ceremony:

"You shall invest him with some of your authority" (Numbers 27:20). Moses laid his hands on Joshua and commissioned him as a successor. As he did, he invested him with his own authority.

A similar story from the Torah about the ordination of the Sanhedrin does not explicitly mention the laying on of hands but implies it:

> Then the LORD said to Moses, "Gather for me seventy men of the elders of Israel ... and I will take some of the Spirit that is on you and put it on them." (Numbers 11:16–17)

The Pharisees taught that Moses ordained Joshua and the seventy elders by laying hands on them. Joshua and the seventy elders in turn ordained their disciples, investing them with the Holy Spirit and the authority that they had received from Moses through the laying on of hands. Their disciples laid hands on the next generation of disciples and so forth—forming a continuous chain of ordination from Moses down to the days of the apostles. This explains why the Master said that the Pharisees and the sages of the Sanhedrin sat in the chair of Moses.

The Talmud describes how Moses received the Torah at Sinai, then passed it on to Joshua, who passed it on to the elders, who passed it on to the prophets, who passed it on to their disciples, who passed it on to the men of the Great Assembly, who passed it on to the sages. The rabbis took this transmission through the laying on of hands seriously because it functioned as an ordination. In those days, a teacher could not serve as a legislator in a Torah court of law, such as the Sanhedrin, unless he had received ordination from previous generations of sages and scholars who had received it from this chain of transmission stretching back to Moses.

CONFERRING THE SPIRIT

The sages taught that those who received the laying on of hands transmitted from Moses also received a portion of the Spirit of God that had rested on Moses. This process began with Joshua, as it says in Deuteronomy 34:9: "And Joshua the son of Nun was full of the spirit of wisdom, for Moses had laid his hands on him." The spirit of wisdom is the Spirit of the LORD. The Spirit also rested upon the seventy elders of the first Sanhedrin:

> Then the LORD came down in the cloud and spoke to him, and took some of the Spirit that was on him and put it on the seventy elders. And as soon as the Spirit rested on them, they prophesied. (Numbers 11:25)

The ritual of ordination through the laying on of hands transfers the Spirit of God from the ordainer to the ordainee. The sages taught that this impartation of the Spirit of God that had been upon Moses gave the sages the wisdom to decide cases, to interpret the Torah, and to teach the Torah with the authority of Moses. To qualify as an elder with the authority to rule on a matter of Torah, one had to have the Divine Spirit that had been upon Moses conferred to him through the laying on of hands. According to the teaching of the Pharisees, an unbroken chain of disciples stretching back to Moses conferred the Spirit that had rested on Moses from generation to generation.

ORDINATION IN THE NEW TESTAMENT

The laying on of hands for the sake of ordination occurs frequently in the New Testament. For example, when the Jerusalem community of Messianic Jews became too large for the twelve apostles to effectively govern, they appointed seven deacons to handle the administration: "These they set before the apostles, and they prayed and laid their hands on them" (Acts 6:6). Through the laying on of hands, the apostles ordained the men, invested the seven deacons with their identity and authority to function as their agents, and conferred blessings upon them.

In another story, when the believers in Antioch decided to send Paul and Barnabas out as their apostles, "they laid their hands on them and sent them off" (Acts 13:3). Through the laying on of hands, the community in Antioch ordained Paul and Barnabas, invested them with their identity to go out as apostles from Antioch, and conferred blessings upon them for the success of the work.

In broader Judaism, judges and elders ordained their successors through the laying on of hands. Likewise among the believers.

The apostles ordained elders over the assemblies with the laying on of hands. Paul told Titus to "appoint elders in every town as I directed you" (Titus 1:5). In the context of a discussion about elders, he warned Timothy, "Do not be hasty in the laying on of hands" (1 Timothy 5:22), perhaps meaning that they should not be too quick to appoint someone as an elder.

IMPARTING AUTHORITY AND THE HOLY SPIRIT

The apostles considered our Master to be the prophet like Moses (mentioned in Deuteronomy 18:18). He is the second Moses, the ultimate Redeemer. Everything about the story of Moses, in one aspect or another, prefigures and foreshadows Jesus.

Moses laid hands upon his disciples, Joshua and the men of the Sanhedrin. He did so to bless them. He did so to invest them with his authority as his legal representatives, not unlike a man laying his hands on the animal that will represent him on the altar or the people laying their hands on the Levites who represent them in the Temple. He invested them with his identity and his authority. When Moses laid his hands upon his disciples, the LORD took the Spirit that was upon Moses and placed it upon Joshua and the elders. He took the authority of Moses and placed it upon Joshua and the elders.

Similarly, Matthew 10 implies that Jesus did the same for his disciples: "He called to him his twelve disciples and gave them authority over unclean spirits, to cast them out, and to heal every disease and every affliction" (Matthew 10:1). How did he do this? Did he just say, "You now have authority"? I believe that he laid hands upon the Twelve.

Moreover, the LORD took from the Spirit that was upon Jesus and distributed it among his followers on the day of Pentecost. Subsequent to that story, the apostles sometimes conveyed the Holy Spirit—transferred the Holy Spirit, so to speak—from themselves to new disciples through the laying on of hands.

For example, when Philip the deacon went to Samaria, many Samaritans believed, but the Holy Spirit "had not yet fallen on any of them, but they had only been baptized [immersed] in the name of the Lord Jesus" (Acts 8:16–17). Simon Peter and John found this puzzling, so they "prayed for them that they might receive the Holy Spirit" (Acts 8:15) and "then they laid their hands on them and they received the Holy Spirit" (Acts 8:17).

The same thing happened to Paul. When Paul arrived in Damascus, the Master sent his disciple Ananias of Damascus to him, "and laying his hands on him he said, 'Brother Saul, the Lord Jesus who appeared to you on the road by which you came has sent me so that you may regain your sight and be filled with the Holy Spirit'" (Acts 9:17).

ANOTHER STORY

Once, Paul encountered some disciples of John the Immerser. He said to them, "'Did you receive the Holy Spirit when you believed?' And they said, 'No, we have not even heard that there is a Holy Spirit'" (Acts 19:2). Paul asked them about their baptism, and they explained that they had been baptized for repentance by John. Paul realized that these disciples of John had never been immersed in the name of Jesus or received the laying on of hands in his name:

> And Paul said, "John baptized with the baptism of repentance, telling the people to believe in the one who was to come after him, that is, Jesus." On hearing this, they were baptized in the name of the Lord Jesus. And when Paul had laid his hands on them, the Holy Spirit came on them, and they began speaking in tongues and prophesying. There were about twelve men in all. (Acts 19:4–7)

This key story demonstrates two important things.

1. The laying on of hands ordinarily followed immediately after baptism.
2. The laying on of hands conferred the Holy Spirit.

When we understand baptism as entrance into Jesus' school of disciples, the follow-up ritual of the laying on of hands makes perfect sense. Disciples of Jesus used the ceremonial laying on of hands to ordain new disciples, just as Moses ordained his disciples.

They used the ceremonial laying on of hands to confer the Spirit that rested upon Jesus to his new disciples, just as Moses conferred the Spirit that rested upon him to his disciples.

The story in Acts 19 presents a definite order of progression from repentance (John's immersion) to instruction to immersion in the name of Jesus to the laying on of hands and receiving the Holy Spirit. Of course, this cannot be a hard and fast rule, and things did not always occur in this order. For example, Paul received the laying on of hands prior to his immersion. Cornelius and his household received the Holy Spirit prior to their immersions. Ordinarily, however, I believe the apostles followed this general progression for new believers:

1. Repentance from dead works
2. Faith toward God through Jesus
3. Instruction about Jesus followed by immersion in Jesus' name
4. The laying on of hands to ordain a disciple and confer the Spirit

TIMOTHY'S ORDINATION

Two passages from the Epistles to Timothy provide further evidence of the function associated with apostolic laying on of hands.

Paul's teaching brought Timothy, his mother Eunice, and his grandmother Lois to faith in Jesus. Paul took Timothy as his own personal disciple and traveling companion. In 1 Timothy 4:14, Paul said to Timothy, "Do not neglect the gift you have, which was given you by prophecy when the council of elders laid their hands on you." I picture this to mean that when Timothy (just a boy at the time) became a believer under the teaching of Paul, he underwent immersion in the name of Jesus. After his immersion, the elders of the community laid hands upon him and prayed over him. They did so as a gesture of blessing, as a father blessing his son. Moreover, they prophesied over him at that time, just as Jacob prophesied over his sons when he laid hands upon them and blessed them. They laid hands on Timothy as a gesture of identification and ordination. They did so to legally pass the impartation of the Holy Spirit that had been upon the Messiah to his new disciple.

Apparently Paul was present when the elders laid their hands on Timothy and prayed for him, receiving him into the school of the disciples of Jesus. Paul said to Timothy:

> I remind you to fan into flame the gift of God, which is in you through the laying on of my hands, for God gave us a spirit not of fear but of power and love and self-control. (2 Timothy 1:6–7)

According to this passage, Timothy received the Spirit of God and a spiritual gift of God at the time that the elders in his community laid their hands upon him and blessed him. God took from the Spirit that had been upon Jesus, and he placed some of that Spirit upon his disciple Timothy.

A STANDARD PROCEDURE

In summary, we set out in this chapter to determine what the book of Hebrews means when it identifies the laying on of hands as one of the basic doctrines of the Messiah. We observed that the Scriptures present us with three different reasons for the ritual:

1. To confer blessing (including healings)
2. To invest identity (including sacrifices)
3. To ordain successors (including disciples)

The apostolic community used elements of all three of these for the purpose of blessing the new disciple, praying for him, prophesying over him, investing Jesus' identity into the new disciple, ordaining the new initiate into his new role as a disciple, and conferring upon him the Holy Spirit.

I am suggesting that the laying on of hands was a standard ritual procedure that new disciples underwent immediately after their immersion. When a new believer completed his period of instruction and emerged from the water, the next step he needed to undergo involved the laying on of hands and the receiving of the gift of the Holy Spirit. Ordinarily, the new disciple received the laying on of hands from one of the apostles, or if not from one of the apostles, from someone who had received it already from one of the apostles, in order to form an unbroken chain of continuity from Jesus to the next generations of his disciples. Along with this ritual (but not because of the ritual), the new disciples received the impartation of the Holy Spirit.

I do not mean to suggest to you that unless someone laid hands on you after your immersion, you did not receive the Holy Spirit. I'm not saying that at all. God's Spirit is not limited by ceremonial concerns like that. I am only suggesting that this was the way it used to happen. I do not think that every time the apostles laid hands on a new believer, a dramatic manifestation of God's Spirit occurred. That's not the point at all. It functioned as more of a legal ceremony, not unlike the ceremonial ordination that the judges and the elders underwent to receive the Spirit of God that had been on Moses before they entered office. The apostolic laying on of hands was not the Pentecostal baptism of the Holy Spirit as much as it was a legal ritual acknowledging a new disciple, receiving a new disciple into the community, blessing the new disciple, praying on his behalf, and asking God to bestow the Spirit upon him.

Back in the days of the apostles, all this must have been basic and obvious to the believers, but we have lost touch with the way that they did things. As Messianic Judaism continues to work toward a restoration of Apostolic-era practice, we should reconsider the ritual of the laying on of hands.

7
THE INITIATION

> Let us leave the elementary doctrine of Christ and go on to maturity, not laying again a foundation of repentance from dead works and of faith toward God, and of instruction about washings, the laying on of hands. (Hebrews 6:1–2)

When I was a young teen, I hesitated to undergo baptism because I was not sure if I was ready to make a permanent commitment to the Christian life. During the first three centuries of our faith, people had better reasons to hesitate. The Roman government considered allegiance to Jesus an illegal superstition. They put both Jews and Gentiles to death for their confession of his name. Going into the water of immersion meant possible arrest, imprisonment, and martyrdom. It required a complete and total surrender of one's future to God's care.

The cost can still be high for Jewish believers—especially when baptism is perceived as renouncing Judaism, the Torah, and the Jewish people and affiliating with a church. When Jewish people realize that the ceremony of "Christian baptism" was originally a form of Jewish immersion, they feel more ownership over the ritual. For example, when the nineteenth-century Hungarian rabbi Isaac Lichtenstein became a believer through his own reading of the New Testament, he famously refused Christian baptism and refused to join any church. He stayed in his post as district rabbi, and he immersed himself into Yeshua's name in a Sabbath mikvah. Around the same era, a young Jewish yeshiva student, also by the name

Lichtenstein (the Even Tzohar, Yechiel Tzvi), was secretly reading the New Testament with a small group of his fellow students. One night the boys went out to a local river and clandestinely immersed themselves into the name of Yeshua.

As a pastor in a Messianic Jewish congregation, I have had the privilege of leading many people, both Jews and (more often) Gentiles, into the water of immersion, including my own children. On one occasion, I had the privilege of bringing a new initiate, a sweet Jewish woman, into the school of discipleship down at the shores of the beautiful Saint Croix River, which flows just a few blocks from our synagogue. At that time, I did not yet know the tradition of fasting before immersion, so I met her and the witnesses for coffee and breakfast at the home of a congregant. Then we went down to a secluded beach with only a handful of people to witness the event. Gray clouds concealed the early morning sunlight, and the sky looked as if it might send forth rain. We stood on the shore, and I read passages from the first Epistle of Peter, as is my custom at immersions. Then I asked the woman the questions of faith, and I asked her if she renounced the work of the devil and confessed Yeshua as the Messiah. At the appropriate time, she strode into the water and quietly recited the traditional blessing for immersion: "Blessed are you, LORD our God, who has sanctified us with his commandments and commanded us regarding immersion in a mikvah." She immersed herself three times, according to the prescribed procedure, and returned to the shore with tears in her eyes. We welcomed her back onto the beach and into the ranks of discipleship. Is anything sweeter than repentance? Is anything better than the name of the Messiah?

A few years later, and after further studies in early Christian sources, our community began to implement a more formal approach to immersion. Now the candidate prepares for several weeks in study and prayer. On the day before the immersion, the candidate fasts in accordance with the instructions in the *Didache*, and several members of the community, who will serve as witnesses at the immersion, undertake the fast with the candidate. The overseeing elder also fasts. We gather around the candidate before the immersion, read scriptures, and offer prayers on his behalf. The candidate recites a traditional confession of sin and makes the statements of faith. After the immersion, the new disciple dons a white garment such as we wear on the Day of Atonement. Then we receive the new initiate into the school of the Master's disciples with prayer and the laying on of hands. We all break the fast with bread and wine, and a celebratory meal follows.

Moreover, our community is now working toward the construction of a kosher mikvah according to the specifications and standards of traditional Jewish law in order to better facilitate this ritual. Even more important than the construction of the new mikvah, however, is the reconstruction of the six elementary teachings that can guide us in the process of ushering new disciples into the kingdom.

RECOVERING THE BASICS

The writer of the book of Hebrews considered the six elementary teachings of Messiah so basic to Christian life that he compared them to milk fed to new believers: "the basic principles of the oracles of God" (Hebrews 5:12) and "the elementary doctrine of Christ" (Hebrews 6:1).

Apparently, he considered the six fundamentals to be so basic that he passed over them with only a brief mention, saying, "Let's leave that stuff behind and not go over it again. Let's go on to more solid material." It's the same story elsewhere in the New Testament. The writers of the New Testament assumed that their readers already knew all these basics. Apparently, the apostles taught the material orally when they first brought the message to people. They wrote their epistles to people who were already believers; they did not write epistles about how to become a believer.

That creates a problem for us. It leaves us trying to recover these basic elementary teachings by reassembling them from the New Testament and other early Christian documents. We are working here to recover the earliest forms of Christian faith. We are trying to uncover the apostolic practice of Messianic Judaism, and in order to do that, we need to do this detective work.

In this chapter, as we continue to reconstruct the elementary doctrine of Messiah, we will pause in our progression through these six teachings to look into three ancient Christian documents—the *Didache*, Justin Martyr's *First Apology*, and the mysterious *Apostolic*

Constitutions—to see how these documents confirm the teachings we have thus far uncovered.

AN INITIATION FOR NEW DISCIPLES

So far, we have examined four of the six elementary teachings and observed that they follow what appears to be, more or less, a progression for new believers: repentance, faith, instruction for immersion, laying on of hands.

The new believer needed repentance from dead works. Dead works are sins. Sins lead to death. The wages of sin is death. A foundation of repentance from dead works calls us to turn away from sin, renounce sin, and submit our wills and our lives to God. This constituted the basic message of Jesus and all his disciples: repent, for the kingdom of heaven is at hand.

Faith toward God implies exercising the fear of the LORD, who rewards righteousness and punishes sin. It demands more than just belief in God; it calls for faith in God based upon the revelation of Jesus, that is to say, belief in the Son sent from the Father to reveal the Father.

Instruction about washings means the catechetical instruction that a believer receives prior to his immersion. We learned from this that in the days of the apostles, prior to immersing someone as a disciple of Jesus, the community ordinarily spent some time teaching the new believer the ways and teachings of Jesus. This was not a hard and fast rule, and we took note of several exceptions, such as the three thousand on Pentecost, the Ethiopian eunuch, and the Philippian jailer, not to mention the household of Cornelius. Under ordinary circumstances, however, a person should know something about what he is getting into prior to undergoing immersion. One should think of his immersion into Messiah as his signature on a contract. A person signing a contract agrees to such and such and so forth, and his signature indicates consent to comply. Before he signs the contract, he wants to know the terms to which he is signing. The Apostolic-era community developed a basic corpus of Jesus' teachings and apostolic expectations that they transmitted to new believers prior to their immersion. We looked at the *Didache* as an example of that catechetical instruction.

In the previous chapter, we did a quick Bible study on the idea of the laying on of hands, and we discovered that in the days of the apostles, the elders of a community (or in some cases, an apostle) laid hands on a new disciple after his immersion. The elder laying hands on the new disciple prayed for him, blessed him, and even prophesied over him. At the same time, he invested Jesus' identity onto the new disciple and ordained the initiate into his new role as a disciple. Most significantly, the laying on of hands conferred the Holy Spirit. We can refer to this ceremony as an investiture, because it invests the new believer with a new identity in Messiah and with the Holy Spirit.

Each of these seems to follow a sequential progression: (1) repent; (2) place your faith in God through Jesus of Nazareth; (3) receive Jesus' teaching and instruction and then immerse yourself into his name for the forgiveness of sins and to signify your entrance into his school of disciples; (4) receive the laying on of hands to confer the Holy Spirit as a sign of the kingdom of heaven and a portion of the Spirit that was upon Jesus.

APOSTOLIC CONSTITUTIONS

An important Christian document called the *Apostolic Constitutions*, perhaps compiled and redacted in the third century, seems to contain material written much earlier than it was assembled. Some of the liturgical material might have roots in the Apostolic Era or shortly thereafter. The *Apostolic Constitutions* provides corroboration for our theory concerning instruction about washings. The *Apostolic Constitutions* seems to make a direct reference to this custom. Read my paraphrase of this short paragraph from the *Apostolic Constitutions*:

> Let the man be instructed regarding the teaching of piety before his baptism: knowledge about the unbegotten God, understanding about the only begotten Son, and full assurance about the Holy Spirit. Let him learn the order of distinctions of creation, the sequence of God's providence, the jurisdiction of different laws, why the world came to be and why God made man to be a citizen of the world. Let him understand his own nature, of what

> sort it is. Let him learn how God punished the wicked by water and fire and glorified the righteous in each generation: I mean Seth, Enos, Enoch, Noah, Abraham and his descendants, Melchizedek, Job, Moses, both Joshua and Caleb, Phinehas the priest, and the holy ones in each generation. [Let him learn] how God, though he foresaw [Adam's sin and the fall of humanity], did not abandon the human race but summoned them at various times from error and folly into an understanding of truth, leading them from slavery and wickedness into freedom and piety, from iniquity into righteousness, from eternal death into everlasting life. Let the one who offers himself [for baptism] learn during his instruction all these things and those that are related to them. (*Apostolic Constitutions* 7.39.2–4)

Unlike the first-century *Didache*, in which the instruction before immersion consisted primarily of the Master's teaching, *Apostolic Constitutions* has the new Christian taking a crash course in biblical literacy and Christian theology. It is interesting that it makes no reference whatsoever to learning the New Testament. This suggests that the tradition we are looking at here predates the canonization of the New Testament, which might imply a date in the late second century.

JUSTIN MARTYR'S FIRST APOLOGY

Let's take a look at Christianity in the middle of the second century by landing our literary time machine around 150 CE during the reign of Antonius Pius, who inherited the Roman Empire from Hadrian shortly after the conclusion of the Bar Kochba revolt.

At this stage in history, a lot has changed from 62 CE, when the book of Hebrews was written. Two Jewish revolts against Rome have brought disaster upon disaster to both Jews and Christians. Rome has unleashed unrelenting persecutions against both. The Temple has been gone for eighty years already. The Jewish people of Judea are now in exile. The apostles are long dead. The Romans have rebuilt Jerusalem as an idolatrous Roman city named Aelia Capitolina. A Temple of Zeus stands on the Temple Mount. A Temple to Venus stands over Golgotha. Gentile Christianity and Judaism have gone through a nasty divorce, which has left both sides bitter and mean-spirited toward the other. The world of the book of Hebrews seems to have completely vanished.

I am describing the world of Justin Martyr, a second-century Christian writer. Justin Martyr's writings provide invaluable information about Christian beliefs and practices in the middle of the second century. He offers the reader something like a snapshot of Gentile Christianity in his day.[2] In his *First Apology*, he explains to Roman readers about the initiation of a new Christian. The following is my own rendition of his description:

> I will also tell about the way in which we dedicated ourselves to God when we were first renewed through Christ, lest, if I skip over this, my explanation [about Christianity] seems incomplete. When a person is persuaded and believes that what we teach and say is true, and he undertakes to be able to live accordingly, he is instructed to pray and to entreat God with fasting, for the remission of his sins from the past, and we pray and fast with him. (Justin Martyr, *First Apology* 61)

Ninety years after the writing of the book of Hebrews, Justin Martyr describes how a new Christian enters the faith. A Roman-era idolater comes into contact with believers. The believers present their views. The idolater finds the message of the gospel persuasive. So he undertakes to live accordingly. This describes repentance from dead works and faith toward God.

Then the new Christian undergoes a period of training, or the instruction about washings. Justin simply says, "He is instructed." This period of instruction concludes with prayer and fasting. Justin says that they do not immerse him until "he has been convinced and assented to the teaching." He explains, "He is instructed to pray and to entreat God with fasting, for the remission of his sins from the past, and we pray and fast with him."

This corresponds exactly to the *Didache* when it says:

2 Justin Martyr, *First Apology* 61, 65–67.

> Concerning immersion, immerse in this way: Having first said all these things [i.e., the instructions in *Didache* 1–6] … Prior to the immersion, the one performing the immersion and the one being immersed should fast beforehand, and also any others if they can. Require the one being immersed to fast one or two days prior to the immersion. (*Didache* 7:1–4, Vine of David translation)

Justin Martyr's second-century description corresponds exactly to the *Didache*'s first-century instructions. The new initiate received instruction prior to immersion and then undertook a fast. The baptizer and the members of the community fasted along with him. Then he was immersed:

> Then we bring him to some place where there is water, and he is regenerated in the same manner in which we ourselves were regenerated. For, in the name of God, the Father and Lord of the universe, and of our Savior Jesus Christ, and of the Holy Spirit, he then receives the washing with water. (Justin Martyr, *First Apology* 61)

And this corresponds very well with the instructions in the *Didache*:

> Having first said all these things, immerse in the name of the Father and the Son and the Holy Spirit in living water. But if you do not have living water, immerse in other water; and if you cannot immerse in cold water, then immerse in warm water. But if you do not have either [in sufficient quantity to immerse], pour water on the head three times in the name of the Father and the Son and the Holy Spirit. (*Didache* 7:1–3)

PRAYERS FOR THE BAPTIZED

Justin Martyr's description conforms to both the *Didache* and the sequence laid out in Hebrews 6:1–2, even with a ceremonial investiture which may have involved the laying on of hands. After the person being immersed came out of the water, the elders led him back to the place of assembly. The Christians gathered there to pray for him. Although Justin does not explicitly say anything about the laying on of hands, he seems to describe the gist of that ceremony. The elders of the assembly prayed over the new initiate and offered prayers for him, which is what happened during the Apostolic Era with the laying on of hands:

> But we, after we have washed him who has been convinced and has assented to our teaching, we bring him to the place where those who are called brethren are assembled, so that we may offer sincere prayers, for ourselves, for the baptized person, and for all others in every place. We pray that we may be counted worthy, now that we have learned the truth, and that by our deeds, we may be found to be good citizens and keepers of the commandments, so that we may be saved with an everlasting salvation. (Justin Martyr, *First Apology* 65)

The *Apostolic Constitutions* also presents a prayer, in liturgical form, for just such an occasion. As you read through my rendition of the prayer below, imagine the scene. We have a freshly immersed new believer, a new Christian, standing before us. He has already repented, has already placed his faith in God and his Messiah, and has already received catechetical instructions before baptism. He has undertaken a personal fast for a day or two. Now he stands before us clothed in white. His hair is still dripping with the water of his immersion. The bishop turns to the congregation and says:

> Let us all sincerely pray to God on behalf of the new initiate. May the One who is good and loves all men hear his prayers and receive his supplications kindly, and may he assist him and grant him the requests of his heart for good, and may he reveal to him the good news of his Messiah, enlighten him and give him understanding, educate him in the knowledge of God, teach him his ordinances and judgments, implant in him the pure and saving fear [of the LORD], open the ears of his heart to engage in his Torah day and night, and may he establish him in piety, unite him with his holy flock and number him with them, grant him the washing of regeneration, the garment of incorruption, the true life, and may he save him from

> all impiety and give place to no adversary against him, and may he cleanse him from all pollution of flesh and spirit, and may he dwell in him, and may he walk with him through his Messiah, and bless his coming in and his going out, and guide his affairs for their good. Let us still sincerely pray for him that, obtaining the remission of his trespasses through this initiation, may he be deemed worthy of the holy mysteries, and of remaining constantly with the righteous.
>
> Now, arise, new initiate, and ask for the peace of God through his Messiah, so that today and the rest of your life will be peaceful and free from sin, and that you will end as a Christian, and that God will be gracious and kind, granting you forgiveness of trespasses.
>
> Dedicate yourself to the only unbegotten God through his Messiah. Bow down and receive a blessing. (*Apostolic Constitutions* 8.6.5–8)

When the bishop instructed the new disciple to "bow down and receive a blessing," this indicates the point in the ceremony at which the bishop and the elders of the community would lay their hands on the head of the new disciple and confer upon him the Holy Spirit that was upon Jesus.

Let's go back to Justin Martyr's description of the ceremony. Justin described a similar scene in which the congregation gathered around the new initiate and offered prayers and blessings on his behalf. A sacred break-fast meal followed the laying on of hands. The new Christian and those fasting with him broke their fast by taking bread and wine together:

> Having finished the prayers, we greet one another with a kiss. Then they bring bread and a cup of wine mixed with water to the president of the brethren (i.e., the bishop). Taking the bread and the wine, he gives praise and glory to the Father of the universe, through the name of the Son and of the Holy Spirit, and he offers a long prayer of thanksgiving for our being counted worthy to receive these things at his hands. And when he has finished these prayers and thanksgivings, all the people present express

> their assent by saying, "Amen." In the Hebrew language, this word, "Amen," means "So be it." When the president has given thanks, and all the people have expressed their assent, those we refer to as servants (deacons) give some of the bread and wine mixed with water over which the thanksgiving was pronounced to each person present, and they carry away a portion to those who are absent. (Justin Martyr, *First Apology* 65)

Justin's description corresponds closely to the *Didache*, which follows up the baptismal instruction with instruction for thanksgiving blessings over the cup and bread.

NOT JUST MAKING STUFF UP

The documents we have examined support our hypotheses about the first four elementary teachings of Messiah, despite the fact that they represent Christian practice in the centuries beyond the Apostolic Era. We see in them repentance, faith in God, catechetical instruction before immersion, a fast before immersion, and immersion into water followed by an investiture ceremony that finally concluded with a sacred meal of bread and wine to break the fast. The tradition seems to have developed and grown from the nascent form reflected in Hebrews 6:1–2, but we can still identify the core elementary teachings of Messiah.

I hope that the historical evidence I am presenting proves that we are not just making stuff up here. Messianic Judaism is not in the business of inventing a new religion, and we are not interested in just playing dress-up Jewish or "let's pretend." In Messianic Judaism, we are doing the hard work of recovering authentic Christian practice—the faith and religion of the first followers of Jesus Christ. I hope that you are starting to get a glimpse of how beautiful, how grand, and how noble our faith is.

8
OUR HOPE IS NOT IN HEAVEN

> Let us leave the elementary doctrine of Christ and go on to maturity, not laying again a foundation of repentance from dead works and of faith toward God, and of instruction about washings, the laying on of hands, the resurrection of the dead. (Hebrews 6:1–2)

So this married couple in their mid-eighties had been married nearly sixty years when, tragically, they perished together in an automobile accident (God forbid). For their advanced age they had been in exceptionally good health, especially during the last two decades of their lives, primarily due to the wife's insistence on a healthy diet and regular exercise.

Saint Peter admitted them through the pearly gates immediately and brought them to their mansion. The estate featured an elegant dining hall, a master bath suite, and an angelic staff of servants. As they admired the palatial home, the man asked Peter how much it was going to cost.

"No charge. It's all free," Peter replied. "This is heaven."

After the tour of the house, Peter brought them out back to see the championship golf course abutting their property line. He told them that they had unlimited golfing privileges and that each week the course changed.

The husband asked, "What are the green fees?"

Peter replied, "This is heaven—you play for free."

They visited the clubhouse and looked over a lavish buffet offering choice cuisines.

"How much is the buffet?" asked the man.

"No charge," Peter replied. "This is heaven—it's all free!"

The man remarked, "Only problem is that I don't see any low-fat or low-cholesterol foods."

Peter said, "That's the best part! In heaven you can eat as much as you like of whatever you like and never gain weight or suffer any adverse consequences."

The man scowled at his wife and said, "You and your broccoli! I could have been here at least ten years ago!"

CONFUSION ABOUT HEAVEN

As I listen to Christians talk about the afterlife and their hope in heaven, I have noticed that there seems to be a great deal of confusion about the entire subject. This confusion began to bother me even when I was a child attending an evangelical church. On the one hand, we taught a straightforward gospel message about believing in Jesus so that people could go to heaven when they died. Going to heaven when we died and trying to get as many other people as we could into heaven when they died was our whole objective. In fact, we defined salvation as a transition from the category of the damned (those who go to hell when they die) into the category of the saved (those who will go to heaven when they die). In this worldview, there are only two types of people, and they are defined by their final destiny: heaven or hell.

In today's world, talk of hell has become increasingly unpopular, to the point at which the mainstream culture has pretty much everyone going to heaven, because after all, wouldn't it be terribly mean and petty of God to punish people? So goes the conventional wisdom.

The popular culture has a vague, fuzzy notion of heaven primarily based on Hollywood's onscreen interpretations of eternal glory and the jumbled reports of people who claim to have had near-death experiences in which they saw a bright light and felt a warm sensation (neurologists explain this as the hallucinatory terrain of a sudden release of a morphine-like drug within the brain associated with the trauma of death). People say ridiculous things such as "Grandpa will always be alive as long as we keep him in our hearts" and recite other such nonsense that reveals that the popular modern expectation of an afterlife consists primarily of outright denial of death.

Therefore, one would expect that if a person wants clarity about what heaven is like, the place to look would be Christianity, which teaches that heaven is our ultimate hope, our goal, our objective, and our eternal home. On the contrary, however, we find that Christianity really has very little clarity to offer on the subject. Before we can go on to discuss the fifth elementary doctrine of Christ, the resurrection of the dead, we need to sift through some of this confusion about the afterlife.

THE CHRISTIAN HEAVEN

In Christian theology, when a Christian dies, he goes to stand in the final judgment, and if he has salvation (whether by the sacraments or by being born again or whatever the prescribed mechanism according to the particular branch of Christian faith to which a person belongs), he then goes on to heaven. Heaven is a place in the sky, beyond the sky, above the clouds. Saint Peter sits at the gates to grant admittance to those whose names are written in the Book of Life because Jesus gave him the keys to the kingdom of heaven (which, by the way, is a complete misunderstanding of that passage and a misunderstanding of the term kingdom of heaven). Pearly gates made of precious stones open onto streets made of gold (which, by the way, is actually borrowed from Isaiah's and John's visions of New Jerusalem on earth, not a description of heaven). Everyone has a mansion of his own (which, by the way, comes from a misunderstanding of the old King James English rendering of John 14:2, which should more accurately be translated "In my Father's house are many dwelling places." The King James English word "mansions" simply meant "dwellings" at the time of that translation, not a palatial house). In heaven there are a lot of people playing harps, since it says in Revelation that people have "harps of God in their hands" (Revelation 15:2).

Beyond those sparse and misconstrued details, nothing seems certain. Many preachers suggest that heaven will be an eternal, never-ending worship service. I imagine one of those charismatic-style song services in which the worship leader keeps doing the same chorus over and over. As my colleague Toby Janicki so accurately quipped, "That sounds more like hell."

This whole concept of heaven is a hard sell, because we are corporeal creatures who are unfamiliar with never-ending states of bliss, and, in fact, we find fulfillment and purpose in meeting challenges, reaching goals, and overcoming conflict. An endless existence without purpose, challenge, goal, or conflict does not sound too exciting. To cap it off, there is no marrying or giving in marriage, so that does not leave much to interest the human mind. I heard one fellow say that he felt relieved to get out of going to hell but was not particularly excited about going to heaven.

On top of all this, we seem to have some uncertainty about whether or not we will recognize loved ones or even remember our lives in the flesh on earth—so I am told, although I am not sure from where that uncertainty comes. In all, the prospect of eternal paradise seems a little flat, and most of the substantive things that people do say about it are from biblical texts taken out of context and misunderstood. There are no pearly gates in heaven. There are no streets of gold. Saint Peter isn't seated at the gate. There are no mansions. And so forth.

Isn't this amazing? I mean, the hope of all hopes, the ultimate goal of Christian confession, the final rest, the hope of glory—so fuzzy and undefined. Christians exhibit a surprising lack of curiosity about heaven, especially considering that much of Christianity today seems to be primarily motivated by the reward of heaven and can be reduced simply to a ticket to heaven. Rarely do we hear sermons about heaven; rarely do people ask about it except to wonder if their pets will be there.

IT'S NOT UP IN HEAVEN

Christianity has muddled, undefined notions of heaven because the Bible almost never talks about heaven. The Bible is not about going to heaven, and originally, in the days of the apostles and the early followers of Jesus, neither was Christianity about going to heaven. Jesus did not come in order to tell people how to go to heaven. He never mentioned how to go to heaven. Moreover, he did not die in order to open the way to heaven.

Before tossing this book in the trash and declaring me a heretic, you should read at least the first two chapters of N.T. Wright's book *Surprised by Hope: Rethinking Heaven, the Resurrection, and the Mission of the Church*. Wright is one of the foremost Christian theologians in the church today, and he makes the same observations I have just noted.

The Bible says very little, almost nothing, about the place we call heaven, and it says even less about how to get there or what to expect when we arrive. Most passages that Christians assume are talking about heaven are not talking about heaven at all. For example, I already mentioned the classic passage in which Jesus says to Peter, "I will give you the keys of the kingdom of heaven" (Matthew 16:19). Christian readers assume that this refers to the keys to the pearly gates that open into the ethereal paradise. It does not. When you read the New Testament in English, through Christian eyes, without knowing anything about Jewish theological idioms and Jewish beliefs, you might come to the conclusion that Jesus and the apostles had lots to say about heaven and how to get into heaven. I'll give you a few examples.

Jesus said, "Blessed are the poor in spirit, for theirs is the kingdom of heaven" (Matthew 5:3), meaning, as many believe, "The poor in spirit will go to heaven." The same applies to those who are persecuted for righteousness: "Theirs is the kingdom of heaven" (Matthew 5:10). Jesus said, "Unless your righteousness exceeds that of the scribes and Pharisees, you will never enter the kingdom of heaven" (Matthew 5:20). In other words, scribes and Pharisees do not go to heaven. Jesus said that we should store up "treasures in heaven, where neither moth nor rust destroys and where thieves do not break in and steal" (Matthew 6:20), meaning that we will one day be able to go to heaven and spend our wealth there so long as we use it charitably here on earth. He said, "Not everyone who says to me, 'Lord, Lord,' will enter the kingdom of heaven, but the one who does the will of my Father who is in heaven" (Matthew 7:21). He said, "Truly, I say to you, unless you turn and become like children, you will never enter the kingdom of heaven" (Matthew 18:3).

The Apostle Paul said, "In this tent we groan, longing to put on our heavenly dwelling" (2 Corinthians 5:2), meaning that in heaven, we will be clothed in a new spiritual form; and "our citizenship is in heaven" (Philippians 3:20), meaning, "We do not belong to this world, we belong to heaven, our real home in the sky." That is, "the hope laid up for you in heaven" (Colossians 1:5) refers to the eternal reward of spending eternity in heaven after death. Paul stated confidently, "The Lord will rescue me from every evil deed and bring me safely into his heavenly kingdom" (2 Timothy 4:18).

I am sorry to be the one to tell you that none of the above Scripture passages mean what they are commonly assumed to mean. That is, none of these passages are about going to heaven when we die.

THE KINGDOM OF HEAVEN

It's easy to see how the church got the wrong impression. Jesus talked about the kingdom of heaven all the time. He sent his disciples out to teach about the kingdom of heaven. The disciples warned people about not entering the kingdom of heaven. Jesus talked about storing up treasure in heaven. The apostles talked about our inheritance in heaven.

Here's the thing about that heaven business. In Judaism, particularly in those days, Jewish people used the word "heaven" as a circumlocution to avoid saying the name of God. Rather than say God's name, they used a variety of substitute words such as heavenly Father, LORD, Most High, Almighty One, Holy One, etc. In addition to these evasive synonyms for God's name and many others, they used the word "heaven" to refer to God.

Let me give you an example. People sometimes express exasperation by saying, "Oh, for God's sake!" This is a shortened version of a fuller sentiment that might mean something along the lines of, "Oh, for God's sake, if not for mine, do shut your mouth and quit talking nonsense!" People shortened these kinds of expressions to the common expletive phrase "Oh, for God's sake!" Since taking God's name in vain like this did not fly in polite company, polite people introduced a circumlocution for the name God, and they said, "Oh, for heaven's sake!" But notice that the word "heaven" stands in for God. A person who says, "Oh, for heaven's sake" actually means, "Oh, for God's sake."

(My mother, of blessed memory, took this circumlocution process a step further and substituted the word "land" as a euphemism for "heaven." I'm sure she did not come up with this innovation herself, but the intention of whoever first did meant "land" to replace "heaven." Rather than saying "Oh, for heaven's sake," which sounds a lot like "Oh, for God's sake," a person substituted the word "heaven" with its opposite, the word "land," in order to further distance himself from profanity. The result is the nonsensical expression "Oh, for land's sake.")

This tendency toward substitution occurred all the time in the Jewish culture of our Master and the apostles. In that regard, the term "kingdom of heaven" does not mean the heavenly abode of angels and disembodied spirits, it functions only as a circumlocution for the term "kingdom of God," which in turn means the Messianic Era. All the Bible's sayings about the kingdom of heaven should be read as "the Messianic Era." This one simple hermeneutical key completely changes the conventional Christian reading of the New Testament. In other words, almost every time it sounds as if Jesus and the apostles were talking about going to heaven, they were actually speaking about the Messianic Era.

WITH GOD

Here is another example. Our Master tells us to store up treasure in heaven. Do you imagine a treasure chest, or a bank account perhaps, waiting for you in heaven, floating on a cloud, where it remains safe from moths and rust and thieves? Jesus said, "Where your treasure is, there your heart will be also" (Matthew 6:21).

That's not what Jesus meant at all. When he said, "Store up treasure in heaven," it meant, "Store up treasure with God." In other words, accumulate merit and reward with the LORD, not on earth. Put your money, your resources, and your efforts into God's work and God's priorities, and then you will have reward from God. We will not find a literal treasure chest or a heavenly ATM machine awaiting us beyond the pearly gates.

Likewise, the apostles said, "Our citizenship is in heaven." This is correct, but it does not mean that we are going to live in heaven. N.T. Wright points out that in the world of the apostles, most Roman citizens did not live in Rome. To say, "My citizenship is in Rome" meant only that you had the privileges of imperial citizenship; it did not mean that you owned a home in Rome or that you were expected to ever settle there.

The apostles spoke of "the hope laid up for [us] in heaven" (Colossians 1:5), which is the same as saying "the hope we have with God." Christians place their hope in God and in his reward for the righteous.

The apostles said that we have "an inheritance ... reserved in heaven" (1 Peter 1:4 NASB), but once again, this means that we have an inheritance with God. It does not mean that we have a piece of land or a mansion in the sky awaiting our incorporeal arrival.

The apostles said, "The Lord will ... bring me safely into his heavenly kingdom" (2 Timothy 4:18), but God's heavenly kingdom will be on earth, not in heaven.

GNOSTIC IDEAS

All this confusion about heaven resulted from our separation from Judaism. When Gentile Christians said, "We don't need Jews or Jewish ideas to understand our own Bible," we started to believe that God has placed our hope—the ultimate hope and the final destiny of Christians—somewhere beyond the sky. Given this amount of confusion about the word "heaven," is it any wonder that Christian ideas about the afterlife come off a little bit muddled?

Christianity has placed all its emphasis on heaven and has held the heavenly goal in antithesis to this world and this life. Because of that, we suffer a dismal, morbid fascination with death, as if rather than being the last enemy to be destroyed, death is a Christian's best friend because it frees him of the shackles of this world of flesh and blood and releases him to go to his real home, his eternal home, in heaven.

That sounds to me like straight-up Gnostic eschatology. Those poor confused second-century heretics called Gnostics believed that physical matter is intrinsically corrupt and evil and that the human body is a cage imprisoning the heavenly spiritual essence of a person. The good news of Gnostics taught that if a person believed the correct things, his soul could be set free and return to its heavenly source, free from the taint of the physical world forever more. That's what the Gnostics taught. Nothing could be more repulsive to the Gnostics than the idea of a physical resurrection into a physical body—a new soul cage.

LIFE AFTER DEATH

I am writing as a bearer of good news to tell you that our hope is not in heaven. If you say, "My hope is in heaven," and by that you mean that your hope is in everlasting life after death in an ethereal paradise inhabited by the disembodied souls of the righteous, then you have misunderstood the gospel. If you say, "My hope is in heaven," and by that you mean that your hope is with God, the one who resides, as it were, in heaven, then you are correct, your hope is with the LORD.

Aside from all this, heaven is real. Pharisaic Jewish theology taught the existence of a paradise for the souls of the righteous. The Pharisees and the apostles believed that when a righteous person dies, his undying spirit separates from his body. Angels come and usher it to paradise, where it joins Abraham, Isaac, Jacob, and all the souls of the righteous in a bounteous garden, so to speak, like Eden. The souls of the righteous bask in the radiance of the Almighty, waiting until that day when they will receive the privilege of reuniting with their bodies at the time of the resurrection of the dead. We do not know much about this paradise of the souls, but we do know that God welcomes those souls back into heaven from whence they originally issued forth.

This paradise of the souls is not, however, the place of life after death. Everyone who goes there is dead. If that was the place of life after death, the people there would be alive, not dead. It's not someplace where we are going to spend eternity. It's not some place with streets of gold and pearly gates, so far as we know. It's not our eternal home. Our home is here, in this world, and in this body of flesh and blood and bone. This is who we are—not a floaty ghost or vapor, not a memory or a dream.

If our hope consisted of attaining a disembodied spiritual state in paradise, it would not be entirely different from most pagan notions of the afterlife. Most pagan cultures hope for an afterlife in which after death, the human spirit leaves the physical body and travels to a realm of ghosts. In those realms of disembodied spirits, they receive some type of either comeuppance or reward for the way they behaved in life. That's a pretty universal human idea. It's hard to imagine that the gospel message had much to contribute to the world if it essentially said the same thing that everyone already believed, namely that there is an afterlife in which human souls have some sort of disembodied existence and deal with the consequences of choices they made during their lives.

That's not the real Christian message, and it is not our hope. We certainly will find consolation in heaven, and we may rest confidently that our loved ones in the Master have departed to that place of light and spiritual joy. As Paul said, "We would rather be away from the body and at home with the Lord" (2 Corinthians 5:8). Beyond any doubt, that's good news, but it's not *the* good news. That is not the message of the gospel that our Master proclaimed.

THE CENTRAL EVENT

All this may come as a surprise to you if you came into the church under the gospel message of "believe in Jesus so that you will go to heaven when you die." I will admit, that's a pretty good incentive for believing in Jesus, especially when the other option involves eternal torment. Once again, and I cannot stress this enough, going to heaven when we die is not the same as entering the kingdom of heaven; it is not life after death, and it is not eternal life. Spending eternity in heaven as a disembodied spirit would be eternal death, not eternal life.

What is this message of eternal life that seems to be so important to the gospel message? If it's not going to heaven when we die, what are we talking about?

I will give you one clue before concluding the chapter: the empty tomb of Jesus of Nazareth. Why was it empty? Was it because his flesh and bones had dematerialized and been replaced by some other spiritual body? No. That did not happen. His hands and feet still bore the wounds from his life on earth. He had the same body. The apostles saw him and touched him and ate with him. He proved to them that he was not a ghost.

The apostles became witnesses to his resurrection. They did not go out proclaiming, "Believe in Jesus who was crucified and on the third day went to heaven." They went out proclaiming, "Believe in Jesus who was crucified and on the third day rose from the dead."

Obviously, the resurrection of Jesus must be the central event of the gospel story. Why is that? What does it mean? And what does it imply for our own futures and the whole concept of life after death?

We need to talk about that in the next chapter, but for now, I can tell you this much: it has everything to do with one of the elementary teachings of the Messiah, those basic doctrines that the apostles considered to be merely the milk of the Word—which is, of course, what we are learning in Hebrews 6: "Let us leave the elementary doctrine of Christ and go on to maturity."

9
THE RESURRECTION OF THE DEAD

> Let us leave the elementary doctrine of Christ and go on to maturity, not laying again a foundation of repentance from dead works and of faith toward God, and of instruction about washings, the laying on of hands, the resurrection of the dead. (Hebrews 6:1–2)

Jewish burials accord the dead sanctity and honor. As the pastor of a Messianic Jewish community, I have been closely involved with the community burial society. The burial society, called a *Chevra Kadisha* (Holy Society), takes care of the body of a deceased brother or sister from the moment of death until burial. We never leave the body unattended. From the moment of death, people take turns sitting on watch beside the body, reading psalms. Before burial, which usually happens within forty-eight hours, a special team assembles to attend to the body. The members of the team begin by ritually immersing themselves in a mikvah. Then they ritually wash the body and dress it in the burial garments, as the disciples did for Tabitha: "When they had washed her, they laid her in an upper room" (Acts 9:37). Likewise, Nicodemus and Joseph of Arimathea prepared the body of Jesus: "They took the body of Jesus and bound it in linen cloths with the spices, as is the burial custom of the Jews" (John 19:40).

The team members place the body in a special wooden casket made without iron or any elements that might impede decomposition. They close the casket. Jewish funerals are never open casket, and there are no wakes. The members of the team conduct these rituals prayerfully and with the utmost solemn respect. Volunteers continue to take shifts, sitting with the casket reading psalms until the funeral, while those who washed the body immerse themselves again. Paul alludes to all these rituals when he asks, "If the dead are not raised at all, why are people baptized on their behalf?" (1 Corinthians 15:29).

At the cemetery, the mourners do not leave the gravesite until the casket has been lowered into the ground. According to custom, each member of the community participates in the burial, taking turns at the shovel to fill the grave, as the disciples did for Stephen: "Devout men buried Stephen and made great lamentation over him" (Acts 8:2).

Sometimes people from other Christian traditions have objected to all this solemn ceremony, saying, "Why do we fuss over the body when the soul is in heaven?" We reply that this body, which we are committing to the earth, will be raised again at the resurrection of the dead, and in light of that ultimate resurrection, we accord the body its due honor.

THE EMPTY TOMB

Our hope is not in heaven. That is to say, our hope for eternal life is not in heaven. The souls in paradise are the souls of the dead, not the living. Most of the Bible passages that Christians ordinarily assume to be about the heavenly paradise of the afterlife are, in fact, not talking about heaven at all. What is this message of eternal life that seems to be so important to the gospel? If it's not about going to heaven when we die, what are we talking about?

To answer that question, we need look no further than the central thing, the most important event in history so far: the empty tomb of Jesus of Nazareth. Why was it empty? Because Jesus had gone to heaven? No, not at all. The tomb was empty precisely because he had not gone to heaven—he was alive, in his own body, and on earth.

When the apostles went out testifying to the resurrection, they did not proclaim the message of a Christ crucified who on the third day went to heaven. They proclaimed Christ crucified who on the third day rose from the dead. The good news is about resurrection—physical, bodily, literal resurrection from the dead. That is the true Christian hope. It is also the Jewish hope and the hope of every disciple of Jesus. This is what we live for, and this is what we die for and why we die fearlessly—the belief that the dead will live again and that death is not the end.

While the apostles said very little about heaven, they talked about the resurrection quite a lot. The resurrection is a component of the kingdom of heaven. It is part of the gospel message, part of the good news.

RESURRECTION, NOT RESUSCITATION

Please note, we are not talking about resuscitation. Prior to the resurrection of Jesus, resuscitations occurred but not resurrections. In our modern world, resuscitation happens every day in modern hospitals. A person's heart stops—the person flatlines. Out come the paddles, and the doctors literally bring people back from the dead. We have an extremely narrow window of opportunity to do this modern miracle, but in principle, this is essentially what happened in the Bible's various stories of people coming back from the dead. For example, Elijah resurrected the son of the widow of Zarephath. Elisha resurrected the son of the Shunamite woman. Our Master resurrected the young man at Nain, the young girl at Capernaum, and his friend Lazarus. All these were, technically speaking, resuscitations. In every instance, the person resuscitated came back to life but only temporarily. Eventually he or she died again.

A resurrection begins similarly to a resuscitation, but it ends differently. When God raises the dead at the end of the age, he will revive their physical bodies and return their souls to those bodies. In the process of that miracle, he will transform those physical bodies so that they cannot die again. They become immortal bodies. The resurrected body will never die:

> We know that Christ, being raised from the dead, will never die again; death no longer has dominion over him. (Romans 6:9)

AN UNPOPULAR IDEA

The belief in literal resurrection does not enjoy much popularity in today's sensible, scientifically sober modern world. The ancient world was even less enthusiastic about the idea. Resurrection defies common sense, medical science, and everything that experience tells us. It's a radical, crazy reversal of what we intuitively feel to be true, namely that when a person dies, he is not coming back to life.

We do not find it so difficult to imagine a spiritual life after death of disembodied souls or of some consciousness set free or returned to its original source. The more vague and abstract, the better and easier to believe. In the days of the apostles, most people believed in that sort of life after death. One need only remember Odysseus' conversation with the moping ghosts in the house of the dead.

Only the Jews, and not all of them, believed in this wild idea of a physical resurrection from the dead. Maimonides lists belief in the resurrection from the dead as one of the basic fundamental principles of Jewish faith. He places it thirteenth in a list of thirteen, not because he considered it the least important, but because it represents the pinnacle and conclusion of Jewish faith. The preceding twelve articles of Jewish faith, including the belief in the coming of the Messiah (number 12), culminate in the resurrection:

> I believe with complete faith that there will be a resurrection of the dead, at the time that the Creator so desires.

According to Maimonides' definition, a form of Judaism that rejects a solid faith in the resurrection of the dead is not really Judaism. One might make the same statement even more emphatically in regard to Christianity. A Christianity that does not believe in a literal, physical resurrection of the dead is not Christianity. Despite this seemingly obvious truism, more and more churches no longer teach a literal resurrection. The mainline Protestant churches have generally abandoned belief in the literal resurrection of Jesus. They explain it as a metaphor for the life of the church that lived on after him. They speak of a spiritual resurrection. They call it a beautiful vision. They call it anything other than a literal, physical resurrection.

In my opinion, that's no longer Christianity. It's something else, something new, but it is not the biblical faith of the followers of Jesus. Paul said, "If there is no resurrection of the dead, then not even Christ has been raised. And if Christ has not been raised, then our preaching is in vain and your faith is in vain" (1 Corinthians 15:13–14). In other words, if there is no literal resurrection of the dead, the whole religion is pointless. He basically said, "If there is no resurrection, we are of all people most to be pitied" (1 Corinthians 15:19).

Authentic biblical teaching on the subject demands a bodily resurrection. What does it even mean to be a human being and to be alive outside of a body? According to the writer of the Epistle to the Hebrews, belief in the resurrection of the dead—not just the resurrection of Messiah but the resurrection of all the dead—is one of the fundamental principles of Messiah. The apostles presented it as one of the basic teachings for new believers: the milk of the faith, that is, an essential, lower-rung teaching.

HERE ON EARTH

The confessing church has never lost the belief in the literal resurrection of Jesus or in a literal resurrection of the dead. The Roman Catholic catechism, for example, presents the case very clearly with no room for wiggling out of it.

The difficulty Christians have struggled with has been the question of how to fit this whole resurrection from the dead thing in with our hope of spending eternity in heaven. The two ideas have never worked well together. In the Bible, the resurrected do not spend eternity in heaven. They spend it here on earth as part of this physical world, which will be renewed in the World to Come. In fact, the whole creation will undergo a resurrection, a transformation, similar to the one that our bodies will undergo. This current world that we live in becomes the World to Come. The Messianic Era transitions humanity from this world to the World to Come.

That is why our hope is not in heaven. Our hope is here on earth (in this world but not of this world) in the Messianic Era and ultimately in the World to Come. The whole world will pass through a rebirth, as the apostle tells us: "Then I saw a new heaven and a new earth, for the first heaven and the first earth had passed away" (Revelation 21:1).

AN OLD ARGUMENT

In the days of the apostles, Judaism suffered great uncertainty over the question of life after death. A large contingency of Jews fell under the influence of Hellenism and rejected the traditional Jewish belief in life after death. The theological leaders of the new progressive interpretations were called Sadducees.

Those who adhered to the philosophy of the Sadducees interpreted prophecies that promise a resurrection or a consciousness beyond the grave as metaphorical. The Pharisees, on the other hand, staunchly defended the existence of the undying soul within man and the revivification of the dead. The bitter divide over this contest of opinion came to the forefront when Paul split the Sanhedrin and hung the jury simply by essentially declaring, "I am on trial because of the resurrection of the dead" (Acts 23:6). The same argument is with us today, no longer as a contest between Pharisees and Sadducees but rather in the divide between secularism and faith.

The argument between the Pharisees and Sadducees amounted to much more than inconsequential theological quibbling. Everything hangs on this question. The argument carried much more gravity than simply speculation about the afterlife; the answer to the question determined whether or not the prophecies of the redemption were literal. Whether or not a person believed in the resurrection had implications for whether or not he believed in the literal coming of a Messiah from the house of David who would usher in the kingdom of heaven and redeem the Jewish people from the nations and establish a new world order of peace. Whether or not a person believed in the resurrection had implications for whether or not he believed that God is just and that he punishes sin and rewards righteousness.

Then it happened. At that very moment in history when the Jewish people had divided over the questions of the existence of an afterlife, the undying soul, paradise and perdition, reward and punishment, and a literal resurrection of the dead, God himself weighed in on the question. He offered his Son, in the person of the man from Nazareth, as the definitive argument to settle the ongoing debate. He sided squarely with the opinion of the Pharisees, proving that their hope was not in vain when he called his Son back from death on the third day after his crucifixion.

TWO RESURRECTIONS

The apostles taught about two distinct resurrection events: a first resurrection and a second resurrection. In the first resurrection, the exiles of Israel and those who are in Messiah will be raised to life, gathered to Messiah, and brought to the kingdom. The second resurrection comes at the conclusion of the kingdom and just prior to the final judgment. All the dead will then be raised. Every human being who has ever lived will come back to life to stand in judgment for deeds they committed in their lives.

According to apostolic teaching, the first resurrection, also called the resurrection of the righteous, will take place at the beginning of the kingdom. The second resurrection, also called the general resurrection, will take place at the end of the kingdom era.

The two resurrections both appear in the basic teaching of Jesus. In John 5:25–27, Jesus speaks about the first resurrection:

> Truly, truly, I say to you, an hour is coming, and is now here, when the dead will hear the voice of the Son of God, and those who hear will live. For as the Father has life in himself, so he has granted the Son also to have life in himself. And he has given him authority to execute judgment, because he is the Son of Man.

Notice that in the first resurrection, the Son gives life to those who hear his voice. This implies that there are others who do not hear his voice and will not come to life at that time. As he says a few verses earlier, "The Son gives life to whom he will" (John 5:21).

He goes on, however, to speak of the general resurrection in John 5:28–29:

> Do not marvel at this, for an hour is coming when all who are in the tombs will hear his voice and come out, those

> who have done good to the resurrection of life, and those who have done evil to the resurrection of judgment.

Revelation 20 also differentiates between two resurrections. Beginning at the end of Revelation 20:4, the apostle describes his vision of the second coming of Jesus:

> They came to life and reigned with Christ for a thousand years. The rest of the dead did not come to life until the thousand years were ended. This is the first resurrection. Blessed and holy is the one who shares in the first resurrection! Over such the second death has no power, but they will be priests of God and of Christ, and they will reign with him for a thousand years. (Revelation 20:4–6)

Now that we have differentiated between two resurrection events, we are prepared to look at a few more passages. We could look at 1 Thessalonians 4:13–18, where Paul says that we should not grieve for the dead as do those with no hope. When the Messiah comes with a shout, the voice of an archangel, and the voice of the shofar of God, the dead in the Messiah will rise and be caught up with him in the clouds to meet him in the air. Those of us still alive at that time will be caught up with him.

When Paul says, "We ... will be caught up together with them in the clouds to meet the Lord in the air" (1 Thessalonians 4:17), he does not mean that we are going to stay in the air, floating on clouds. Messiah comes to gather the exiles to bring them with him to the Holy Land, as the prophets have predicted, and they arrive there carried upon the clouds. He does not rapture the resurrected up to heaven; rather, he carries them to Jerusalem. "He who raised the Lord Jesus will raise us also with Jesus and bring us with you into his presence" (2 Corinthians 4:14).

Jewish funeral rites accord special honor to the body because the body will be raised again. Judaism does not practice cremation. Both Jews and Christians bury the dead because of their hope in resurrection. Many pagan cultures, by contrast, burned the corpses of the dead in a heathenish funeral bonfire.

THE MARTYRS FROM LYONS

N.T. Wright's book *Surprised by Hope* offers the story of the martyrs of Lyons as an example of early Christian hope in the resurrection. The second-century church father Irenaeus described the terrible persecution against the Christians of Lyons that took place in his lifetime. He described how the Romans tortured the Christians and put them to grisly deaths. Then they burned their bodies, reducing them to ashes, and swept the ashes into the River Rhone so that no trace of them might remain on earth. Irenaeus says, "They did this to prevent their new birth, that, as they said, 'They may have no hope of a resurrection, through trust in which they bring to us this foreign and new superstition, and despise terrible torments, and are even ready to go to death with joy. Now let us see if they rise again.'"

> Someone will ask, "How are the dead raised? With what kind of body do they come?" You foolish person! What you sow does not come to life unless it dies. And what you sow is not the body that is to be, but a bare kernel. … But God gives it a body as he has chosen, and to each kind of seed its own body. (1 Corinthians 15:35–38)

In other words, the resurrection of the dead does not require our body to be intact. It requires only a fragment, a seed, so to speak, and this is what modern genetics tells us as well. We could create spare bodies right now from our DNA. We have the technology. The rabbis taught that the human body contains a tiny, indestructible bone called the *luz*, which God will use to resurrect people. Medical science tells us that no such bone exists, but if we understand the *luz* bone to refer to a person's genetic sequence, the ancient explanation still stands.

The martyrs from Lyons will rise again, despite the best efforts of the Romans.

WHAT KIND OF BODY?

What will we be like when we are raised? The rabbis discussed this question frequently. They said that we will each be resurrected with our own body. They supposed that God will raise us up with the same disabilities and handicaps that we had in life but that the LORD will heal us. The resurrection of Jesus shows us that the Master still wore the wounds of his crucifixion, proving the risen body is the same body:

> "See my hands and my feet, that it is I myself. Touch me, and see. For a spirit does not have flesh and bones as you see that I have." And when he had said this, he showed them his hands and his feet. (Luke 24:39–40)

Although God will raise us into the same bodies, these bodies will be transformed into an immortal, imperishable state like that of the resurrected Messiah:

> We shall certainly be united with him in a resurrection like his. (Romans 6:5)

> What we will be has not yet appeared; but we know that when he appears we shall be like him, because we shall see him as he is. (1 John 3:2)

> If the Spirit of him who raised Jesus from the dead dwells in you, he who raised Christ Jesus from the dead will also give life to your mortal bodies through his Spirit who dwells in you. (Romans 8:11)

> We … are being transformed into the same image from one degree of glory to another. (2 Corinthians 3:18)

> So is it with the resurrection of the dead. What is sown is perishable; what is raised is imperishable. It is sown in dishonor; it is raised in glory. It is sown in weakness; it is raised in power. It is sown a natural body; it is raised a spiritual body. If there is a natural body, there is also a spiritual body. (1 Corinthians 15:42–44)

Apostolic theology teaches that all human life came through Adam, the first man. So too, all new life in the resurrection comes through Messiah, the heavenly Adam. In other words, the resurrection of Messiah marked a new beginning for the whole human species. Paul called Messiah the "firstfruits of those who have fallen asleep" (1 Corinthians 15:20). The first Adam came from the dust, and our mortal bodies are merely so much dust. The heavenly Adam, however, is spiritual:

> Just as we have borne the image of the man of dust, we shall also bear the image of the man of heaven. I tell you this, brothers: flesh and blood cannot inherit the kingdom of God, nor does the perishable inherit the imperishable. (1 Corinthians 15:49–50)

The perishable, mortal body must be transformed into an imperishable, immortal body. When that happens, "Death is swallowed up in victory" (1 Corinthians 15:54).

The doctrine of the final resurrection reminds us again of what we are, of the fact that a human person is not simply a spirit. A resurrected human being includes the whole person, the human body quickened with the Spirit.

ALL THINGS NEW

The resurrection of the dead will happen in the future, but it has implications for today.

The resurrection of Messiah is good news, because it means that the kingdom is at hand and that all the prophecies of the redemption of Israel will be fulfilled. The resurrection of Jesus vouches for the theological tenets of Pharisaism, all of which Jesus himself espoused and endorsed. For those of us who accept that Jesus rose from the dead, this is the most important thing in the world, because it shapes everything we believe, everything for which we live, and everything for which we hope. Confidence in the resurrection changes our whole life, our outlook on life and death, and the way we live our lives—at least it should if we follow the logic. In fact, the resurrection of Jesus goes one further and demands the existence of God himself. To accept the premise that Jesus literally rose from the dead requires accepting the whole package of biblical truth and the message of the kingdom.

In the Messiah, even now on earth, every believer participates in the resurrection. Paul said, "Consider yourselves dead to sin and alive to God in Christ Jesus" (Romans 6:11). We live in the kingdom today, so to speak, by counting ourselves dead to sin and transformed already into the new life. In this regard, the doctrine of the resurrection has practical, ethical ramifications for the believer.

The doctrine of the resurrection should encourage us to take care of these mortal bodies as best we can. We should not disregard this body as if it is unimportant, like a garment to be shed, because it is in fact the body that will be raised from the dead. This garment will not be shed to be disposed of but to be remade. Therefore, as a matter of dignity and honor for the body, we should take care of our body's physical needs, and this includes avoiding things that damage our health and pursuing those things that promote good health.

The doctrine of the resurrection gives us eternal hope. Like those martyrs of Lyons and like the men and women of faith listed in Hebrews 11, we have no fear of death, because we have confidence in life after death. We do not fear those who can destroy only the body, whether they be Roman persecutors or malignant cancer cells.

The resurrection of the dead implies that we are not just animals.

Life is not "Eat, drink, and be merry, for tomorrow we die" (1 Corinthians 15:32), which is hedonism, nor is it "Life is difficult, and then you die," which is nihilism. We are not just complex biological machines. We are not just going through the motions like rats running the cosmic maze. We have an eternal undying soul of inestimable value—a transcendent being designed to live on and preserve our person when our body fails, and that is ultimately destined to be returned to our body.

> My God, the soul that you placed in me is pure. You created it, you formed it, you breathed it into me, and you guard it within me, and you will ultimately lift it away from me, only to return it to me in the future to come. For the entire time that my soul is within me, I give thanks to you, O LORD, my God and God of my fathers, Great One over all works, Master of all souls. Blessed are you, O LORD, who returns souls to dead bodies. (*Siddur*)

This eternal life can live within us today and inform us today to inspire us to greatness. Abraham Joshua Heschel said that a person should not regard his life as that of an animal but rather should think of it as a work of art, made by design with intention, with beauty, and with purpose. When the inevitable end of life does come, it is not the end.

The resurrection of Jesus indicates not only our own restoration and the resurrection of human beings but a restoration of the entire creation, a resurrection of heaven and earth, which will be transformed into a new heaven and a new earth: "And he that sat upon the throne said, Behold, I make all things new" (Revelation 21:5 KJV). The whole creation groans in anticipation of this transformation, restoration, and resurrection.

Come, Lord, and tarry not;
Bring the long-looked-for day;
O why these years of waiting here,
These ages of delay?

Come, for thy saints still wait;
Daily ascends their sigh.
The Spirit and the Bride say, "Come":
Dost Thou not hear the cry?

Come, for creation groans,
Impatient of thy stay,
Worn out with these long years of ill,
These ages of delay.

Come, and make all things new;
Build up this ruined earth;
Restore our faded Paradise,
Creation's second birth.

Come, and bring thy reign
Of everlasting peace;
Come, take the kingdom to thyself,
Great King of Righteousness.

(Horatius Bonar, 1846)

10
THE ETERNAL JUDGMENT

> Therefore let us leave the elementary doctrine of Christ and go on to maturity, not laying again a foundation of repentance from dead works and of faith toward God, and of instruction about washings, the laying on of hands, the resurrection of the dead, and eternal judgment. (Hebrews 6:1–2)

During his tenure as governor over Judea, the reprehensible Roman governor Felix dealt in corruption, bribery, assassinations, and all manner of injustice, but that was only normal for a Roman governor. What made Felix truly culpable to the Jewish people was his marriage to his wife, the beautiful Princess Drusilla. She was the youngest daughter of the celebrity-king Herod Agrippa the first, who had died young and at the height of his popularity. "An angel of the Lord struck him down, because he did not give God the glory, and he was eaten by worms and breathed his last" (Acts 12:23). He left behind three daughters and a son.

Drusilla, the youngest, was six years old at the time of her father's death, but she blossomed to become a legendary beauty; eclipsing her sisters, she became, in the words of Josephus, the most beautiful of all women. She was married young to an important king from Syria who converted to Judaism just to be married to the beautiful Drusilla, the Jewish princess. Then the reprehensible Felix laid eyes on her and determined to take her for himself. How did he do it? He hired a wicked sorcerer to use his arcane arts and powers of persuasion on the young bride, enchanting her and, at length, convincing her to abandon her husband, the king, and to run off with Felix. She moved into her great grandfather Herod's palace in Caesarea and became the wife of a Gentile. The marriage embarrassed and scandalized the Jewish world. I have to imagine that when she came to her senses, Drusilla must have been terribly ashamed. She seems to have been seeking some path of repentance.

Sometime into the marriage, her husband, Felix, told her about a curious court case involving a Jew accused by the Jewish authorities of various crimes. The prisoner, a man named Paul, believed in a dead man who had come back to life. Drusilla recognized him for a disciple of Jesus, and she said she wanted to hear him:

> After some days Felix came with his wife Drusilla, who was Jewish, and he sent for Paul and heard him speak about faith in Christ Jesus. And as he reasoned about righteousness and self-control and the coming judgment, Felix was alarmed and said, "Go away for the present. When I get an opportunity I will summon you." (Acts 24:24–25)

We do not know if Drusilla got the message or repented, but it sounds as if Felix understood Paul's message all too well. Why did Paul's words so frighten and alarm Felix the Roman?

THE ETERNAL JUDGMENT

In the previous chapter, we studied the fifth elementary doctrine of Christ, the resurrection of the dead. We learned that our hope is not in heaven but rather here on earth in a new body, which will be raised when the Holy One, blessed be he, chooses to awaken the dead. We learned that apostolic eschatology expected two different resurrection events: a first resurrection and a second resurrection. The first resurrection, also called the resurrection of the righteous, initiates the Messianic Era. The second resurrection, also called the general resurrection, occurs at the point of transition from this world to the World to Come. Then comes the "eternal judgment," which is the sixth and last of the elementary teachings listed in Hebrews 6:1–2.

The eternal judgment is the sixth and final step on this journey and the final step on every journey. The writer of the book of Hebrews says, "It is appointed for man to die once, and after that comes judgment" (Hebrews 9:27).

JESUS ON THE FINAL JUDGMENT

The final judgment occupies an important place in the teachings of our Master and the apostles. Our Master's teachings are closely linked to the idea of preparing for this final judgment. Almost everything he says has an eye toward it. Read through the following montage of judgment-day teachings from the words of Jesus:

> Cast the worthless servant into the outer darkness. In that place there will be weeping and gnashing of teeth. (Matthew 25:30)
>
> When the Son of Man comes in his glory, and all the angels with him, then he will sit on his glorious throne. Before him will be gathered all the nations, and he will separate people one from another. (Matthew 25:31–32)
>
> Then he will answer them, saying, "Truly, I say to you, as you did not do it to one of the least of these, you did not do it to me." And these will go away into eternal punishment, but the righteous into eternal life. (Matthew 25:45–46)
>
> So it will be at the end of the age. The angels will come out and separate the evil from the righteous and throw them into the fiery furnace. In that place there will be weeping and gnashing of teeth. (Matthew 13:49–50)
>
> Truly, I say to you, it will be more bearable on the day of judgment for the land of Sodom and Gomorrah than for that town. (Matthew 10:15)
>
> But I tell you, it will be more bearable on the day of judgment for Tyre and Sidon than for you. (Matthew 11:22)

> The men of Nineveh will rise up at the judgment with this generation and condemn it. ... The queen of the South will rise up at the judgment with this generation and condemn it. (Matthew 12:41–42)

> I tell you, on the day of judgment people will give account for every careless word they speak. (Matthew 12:36)

> Just as the weeds are gathered and burned with fire, so will it be at the end of the age. The Son of Man will send his angels, and they will gather out of his kingdom all causes of sin and all law-breakers, and throw them into the fiery furnace. In that place there will be weeping and gnashing of teeth. Then the righteous will shine like the sun in the kingdom of their Father. He who has ears, let him hear. (Matthew 13:40–43)

JUSTICE IN THIS LIFE OR THE NEXT?

In the days of the apostles, Jewish people had different opinions on this subject. Most fell into one of two schools of thought. The Sadducean theologians taught that God dispenses justice only in this world. In other words, a person received whatever he deserved within the span of his lifetime on earth. When people suffered, that was a clear sign that for some reason they deserved to suffer. When people succeeded or enjoyed wealth, that indicated that they deserved it. If they did not deserve it, they could expect a reversal of circumstance within their lifetime, because God's justice repays each person for what he deserves. Final justice happens in this lifetime. Bad things happen to bad people. Good things happen to good people. God might let bad things happen to good people as a temporary testing, but eventually good things will happen to them, unless they really actually do deserve the bad. That's how the Sadducean thinking goes, I suppose.

The Pharisees had a different take on this subject. They did believe, like the Sadducees, that people received justice for their deeds in this life, but they also believed that the ultimate judgment takes place not in this lifetime but in the afterlife. God dispenses his ultimate punishments and rewards after death in Gehenna and Paradise, and finally, after the resurrection, when a final day of judgment will assign reward or punishment to each man according to the deeds he committed while alive. The righteous will be rewarded, but the wicked will go into everlasting darkness.

This means that in Pharisaic theology, a person might not get everything he deserves in this lifetime. There might be considerably more suffering and punishment stored up for the wicked after their deaths, and considerably more reward and consolation reserved for the righteous to be paid out to them after their deaths.

THE BOOKS OF JUDGMENT

Jewish tradition teaches that the heavenly court opens three books: the Book of Life for the righteous, the book of death for the wicked, and the book of the intermediates for the intermediate. Everyone's name will be written in one of the three books. Those whose names are written in the Book of Life will be assigned to life in the World to Come. Those whose names are written in the book of death will be assigned to eternal damnation. Those whose names are written in the book of the intermediates, who are neither righteous enough to merit eternal life nor wicked enough to merit eternal damnation, must stand in judgment before the heavenly court. The heavenly court reviews their cases, considering the merits and demerits of each individual, and finally assigns each of these people into either the Book of Life or the book of death.

THE HIGH HOLIDAYS

In Messianic Judaism, we rehearse for this final judgment every year in the high holidays of Rosh HaShanah and Yom Kippur (Festival of Trumpets and Day of Atonement). Judaism treats the high holidays as an annual dress rehearsal for the final eternal judgment. In anticipation of the holidays, we repent, confess sins, mend relationships, apologize, and try to make peace with both men and God.

According to the tradition, the festival of Rosh HaShanah convenes the court and opens the books. The festival of Yom Kippur, ten days later, adjourns the court and issues the verdicts.

This does not mean that Rosh HaShanah and Yom Kippur are the final judgment. They foreshadow the final judgment, but God does not judge souls for eternal life or damnation on the high holidays. Instead, tradition says that he judges us at the high holidays for life in this world. The heavenly court reviews our deeds and decides if we will live for another year. If we will live, what fortunes will befall us? Will we be wealthy or poor, healthy or sick? All this is decided during the high holidays. If we do not merit life for another year, the court records our names in the book of death.

Again, the high holidays are not supposed to be imagined to be the eternal judgment. They symbolize a temporal judgment.

TEMPORAL VERSUS ETERNAL

Temporal judgments refer to things that happen in this world within this lifetime. A temporal judgment involves consequences for sins in this world. It's the only type of judgment that the Sadducees believed in. Most temporal judgments in the Bible tend to be national. For example, the blessings and curses in the Torah are examples of temporal judgments that befell the whole nation. Our Master taught about temporal judgments too. He warned of the coming destruction of Jerusalem and the exile. Devastating as those judgments were, they were temporary judgments that can, and will, be reversed. Most of the strokes of judgment that we read about in the prophets refer to temporal judgments. They fall upon the nation as a whole and upon individuals. They provide evidence of God's ongoing involvement in this current world.

Eternal judgment, on the other hand, refers to one final judgment. The individual, not the whole nation, stands in judgment. This judgment takes place not in this world but in the next. In the final eternal judgment, each human being stands before the throne of judgment to receive a final eternal, everlasting verdict.

ETERNAL JUDGMENT IN DANIEL

Our Master spoke a great deal about the eternal judgment. His teaching came back to the macabre subject again and again. He saw himself personally as taking on a significant role in this final judgment.

Jesus seems to have relied on Daniel 7 as a programmatic text on the subject of the eternal judgment. In this passage, the prophet Daniel received an apocalyptic vision of the times to come—a peek into the future. The LORD gave him dreams and visions about the future and the end of time:

> As I looked, thrones were placed, and the Ancient of Days took his seat; his clothing was white as snow, and the hair of his head like pure wool; his throne was fiery flames; its wheels were burning fire. A stream of fire issued and came out from before him; a thousand thousands served him, and ten thousand times ten thousand stood before him; the court sat in judgment, and the books were opened. (Daniel 7:9–10)

Before reading any further in Daniel 7, pause to take in Daniel's vision of the final judgment. The Ancient of Days is seated. Thousands of angels flow forth like a river of fire to serve him. Ten thousand times ten thousand people waiting for their verdicts stand before him. The heavenly court is seated. Books of judgment are opened.

Suddenly, "one like a son of man" steps forward to deliver the sentencing:

> I saw in the night visions, and behold, with the clouds of heaven there came one like a son of man, and he came to the Ancient of Days and was presented before him. And to him was given dominion and glory and a kingdom, that all peoples, nations, and languages should serve him; his dominion is an everlasting dominion, which shall not pass away, and his kingdom one that shall not be destroyed. (Daniel 7:13–14)

THE SON OF MAN IN JUDGMENT

Jesus' own self-identity and understanding of Messiah centered on this important passage from Daniel. He understood the term "one like a Son of Man" as a title for the Messiah, and he believed himself to be that Son of Man.

The apocryphal book of Enoch, a favorite among first-century Jewish readers, developed this messianic Son of Man Christology further. The book of Enoch equated the heavenly Son of Man with the Davidic Messiah, the anointed branch from the house of Jesse predicted in Isaiah 11. According to 1 Enoch, the LORD will entrust the Son of Man with judgment over all nations in the end of days. He will become the agent of God's will on earth and God's agent in the resurrection of the righteous. The LORD will give the sum of the final judgment over to him:

> And he sat on the throne of his glory, and the sum of judgment was given unto the Son of Man. And he caused the sinners to pass away and be destroyed from off the face of the earth, and those who have led the world astray. With chains shall they be bound, and in their assemblage-place of destruction shall they be imprisoned, and all their works vanish from the face of the earth.
>
> And from henceforth there shall be nothing corruptible; for that Son of Man has appeared, and has seated himself on the throne of his glory, and all evil shall pass away before his face. And the word of that Son of Man shall go forth and be strong before the Lord of Spirits. This is the third Parable of Enoch. (1 Enoch 69:27–29)

These passages provide us the background for John 5:22–30, a text we looked at in the previous chapter. While speaking about his participation in the future resurrection of the dead, Jesus said that the Father himself judges no one because he delivers all judgment to the Son. He added, "I can do nothing on my own. As I hear, I judge, and my judgment is just, because I seek not my own will but the will of him who sent me" (John 5:30).

JUDGMENT SEAT OF MESSIAH

A final judgment is coming for every human being. The wicked and the righteous and the intermediate will all be raised to stand in judgment. The Messiah himself will preside as the judge, acting as the agent of his Father:

> For we must all appear before the judgment seat of Christ, so that each one may receive what is due for what he has done in the body, whether good or evil. Therefore, knowing the fear of the Lord, we persuade others. (2 Corinthians 5:10–11)

In these words, Paul expressed his motive for evangelism: "Therefore, knowing the fear of the Lord, we persuade others." Paul knew the fear of the LORD. To fear God is to believe that he exists, rewards, and punishes. Paul knew that eventually God will judge the wicked and reward the righteous. He taught that we must all stand before the Messiah in the final judgment. When we do, we will face the judge, and we will need to look him in the eye and receive what is due us for what we have done, whether good or evil.

Paul the Pharisee believed that this eternal judgment was lying in store for every person, whether he knew it or not, so he spent his life trying to persuade people to prepare for it by repenting now, in this life, by seeking forgiveness from the judge before it was too late. He urged people to make peace with God, now in this life, by finding forgiveness and righteousness through the Messiah.

The shadow of punishment and the hope of reward in the final judgment permeate all the teachings of the New Testament. Whether we are learning from Jesus in the Synoptic Gospels, discussing the Son of Man sitting on his glorious throne and judging the nations, learning from Jesus in the Gospel of John about eternal life, spending time with Paul as he fusses over justification, faith, and righteousness, or spending time with Peter, James, or Jude or with John in his Epistles or in the book of Revelation, the anticipation of the final judgment runs through it all and ties it all together.

And of course, the gospel message offers the great hope that in the name of Yeshua of Nazareth, those who repent from sins committed in the flesh can find forgiveness for those sins and have them removed from the books, so to speak, before facing the final judgment. Evangelicals call it getting saved.

NOT A POPULAR SUBJECT

One hears more invitations to heaven than warnings about hell.

Most Christian notions of hell consist of a puzzling muddle of ideas collected from mismatched Bible passages, resulting in the mistaken notions that hell consists of underground passages in the earth in which Satan and all his devils abide, tormenting the souls of the damned. In today's postmodern world, the whole concept sounds like a nightmare from mythology or a hangover from the Middle Ages. It's a good subject for jokes and comic strips, but no one takes hell very seriously.

Generally speaking, the doctrine of the eternal judgment has fallen into disfavor. Perhaps this shift in emphasis from everlasting punishment to a blissful afterlife occurred as a natural swing of the theological pendulum. The medieval and Reformation-era church had an unhealthy fascination with the torments of hell. Evangelicals later demonstrated the same fixation, predicating their appeal for the gospel on the basis of avoiding damnation. The church framed Christianity primarily as an avenue of escape from everlasting fiery tortures and the pitchfork of Satan. We substituted the foundational doctrine of eternal judgment for the doctrine of eternal damnation.

The apostolic doctrine of eternal judgment is not the same as the Christian doctrine of eternal damnation. The apostles teach that the judgment has not yet taken place and will not take place until the end of time. Most Christians seem to assume that it has already happened and that they themselves are commissioned to announce the verdicts. (Pretty much everyone but them goes to hell.)

In apostolic theology, the doctrine of eternal judgment did not function as a threat with which to frighten people into the kingdom. Instead, the early disciples saw it as a promise of hope that in the end everything will work out right, because God is going to reward each man according to his deeds. Although the righteous and the innocent might suffer in this world, they will find reward in the World to Come. Although the wicked might seem to prosper and live full and happy lives in this world while they victimize the weak and perpetrate injustices, they will get what they have coming in the end.

Confidence in the ultimate justice of God inspired the apostles and their followers to fearlessly face down injustice and persecution. They patiently suffered ignominy and imprisonment under man's crooked systems of justice because they had confidence in the final judgment. They willingly sacrificed their own comforts and pleasures in this world because they looked forward to the reward of the next.

THE FINAL VERDICT

The eternal judgment is so basic and fundamental to our faith that the writer of the book of Hebrews considers it to be the milk. It is pretty simple. We believe that every human life has eternal significance—so much so that the deeds committed in this body will have ramifications that completely transcend time. That makes every moment of this life precious. It makes every opportunity to perform a good work (mitzvah) precious. It makes every sin utterly abhorrent. Every righteous deed merits eternal reward, and every sin earns eternal punishment. Ironically, the doctrine of the eternal judgment makes life in this temporary world all the more significant.

The down side, of course, is that darn book of death. What if you find yourself standing before the judgment and are exposed as a sinner? The prosecuting attorney will be there to point out all your selfishness, your pettiness, your foolishness, your many, many sins, most of which you had forgotten.

The hope of the gospel teaches that those who repent from dead works in the name of Jesus, have faith toward God through the Messiah, are instructed and immersed into Jesus, receive the laying on of hands in the name of Jesus, and are raised from the dead by the voice of Jesus need not fear condemnation in the eternal judgment, for we have already died with him and been raised with him, and we abide in him and rely on him. What a relief it will be, on the day we stand before the terrifying judge, to look him in the eye and see the spark of recognition.

SNAPSHOT OF THE FINAL JUDGMENT

What was it that so frightened Felix the Roman that he sent Paul away? What was Paul saying about "righteousness, self-control, and the coming judgment" that alarmed Felix?

It was probably something along the lines of what we read in 2 Peter 3 and the last verses of Revelation 20.

"The heavens and earth that now exist are stored up for fire, being kept until the day of judgment and destruction of the ungodly" (2 Peter 3:7). When the Son of Man comes with all his angels and sits upon his glorious throne, earth and sky will flee, and no longer will any place be found for them. "Then the heavens will pass away with a roar, and the heavenly bodies will be burned up and dissolved, and the earth and the works that are done on it will be exposed" (2 Peter 3:10). As the elements melt and this world collapses all around us and the stars explode and all matter dissolves into pure energy, behold, all the dead will be summoned.

A voice will say to the sea, "Give up your dead," and all those who perished at sea or whose bodies were washed out to sea or who were sunk beneath the waves will come forth to stand in judgment, and there will be no more sea. A voice will say to the earth, "Give up your dead," and all those who are buried in the earth will rise and come forth, and there will be no more earth. A voice will say to Sheol, "Give up your dead," and all the souls in that place will be released and returned to their bodies.

Then you will see the dead, great and small, famous and obscure, those who lived full lives and those who did not, the primitive and the civilized, the enlightened and the ignorant, the religious and the secular, every race and religion, all peoples, nations, and languages, every family, all human history, gathered together in one place at one time outside of place and time, standing before the Ancient of Days. He will be seated on the throne, his clothing white as snow, the hair of his head like pure wool, his throne fiery flames, its wheels of burning fire, and a stream of fire issuing forth from before him.

Then the books will be opened. And another book will be opened, which is the Book of Life. And the dead will be judged by what is written in the books, according to what they have done, according to how they exercised righteousness and self-control and showed concern for others and acted honorably and decently or shamefully and wantonly.

We call this scene the last judgment and the final judgment, because it brings the closing scene on the drama of human events and their moral consequences. We call it the eternal judgment, because its verdicts are final and forever.

Then death will be thrown into the lake of fire, and there will be no more death. Then Sheol will be thrown into the lake of fire, and there will be no more Sheol. And if anyone's name is not found written in the Book of Life, he will be thrown into the lake of fire with death and Sheol. Then behold the new heaven and the new earth, for the first heaven and the first earth will pass away, and the sea will pass away, for he will make all things new.

> Since all these things are thus to be dissolved, what sort of people ought you to be in lives of holiness and godliness, waiting for and hastening the coming of the day of God, because of which the heavens will be set on fire and dissolved, and the heavenly bodies will melt as they burn! But according to his promise we are waiting for new heavens and a new earth in which righteousness dwells. Therefore, beloved, since you are waiting for these, be diligent to be found by him without spot or blemish, and at peace. And count the patience of our Lord as salvation. (2 Peter 3:11–15)

11
ON TO MATURITY

> Therefore let us leave the elementary doctrine of Christ and go on to maturity. (Hebrews 6:1)

In retrospect, the six foundations are all obvious tenets of New Testament theology. Because they are so obvious and rudimentary, the New Testament writers did not feel compelled to spell them out. The apostles conveyed these basic teachings orally to their students, and new disciples learned them as a sort of apostolic catechism prior to being received into Jesus' school of disciples.

The initiation worked well enough until Christianity slipped away from its Jewish moorings. Outside of its original Jewish context, these basic institutions and doctrines began to evolve and adapt into completely new forms. Later generations of Christians no longer remembered the basics.

In the context of the Epistle to the Hebrews, the six foundations of the elementary doctrine of Messiah receive only passing notice. The writer of the epistle urges his readers on to deeper waters. He says, "Let us leave the elementary doctrine of Christ and go on to maturity, not laying again a foundation … and this we will do if God permits." He implies that with the foundations of the elementary teaching properly laid, we are able to go on to maturity. A schoolchild cannot learn algebra until he has mastered arithmetic. Neither can a believer find spiritual maturity if he has not mastered the basic teaching of Messiah.

Believers today are seldom identified with spiritual maturity.

Our lack of maturity indicates that the time has come for us to be "laying again a foundation." I believe that this is a matter of survival. Anyone who seriously cares about whether or not we leave behind us a credible testimony to the gospel that can point the way for the next generation should be about the business of rebuilding on the original foundations. We have tottered so far off those foundations that the entire structure leans toward collapse.

The Christian church today seems ill-suited to survive the postmodern era's ideological storms and rising flood of secularism. Jesus warned us about the consequences of building our house on sand.

Many Christian leaders have recognized the urgent need to establish solid foundations, but the basic principles they have chosen to build upon are not the ones selected by the apostles. Fundamentalists and evangelicals fight bravely to defend against the rising floods. They cling to the higher ground of scientific creationism, biblical inerrancy, heterosexuality, and the deity of Jesus. Reformed theologians shore up their five points of doctrine and practice their rhetorical skills. Others work overtime to patch the cracking foundations of the particular systems of dogma they have inherited through their denominational traditions. No one notices the still, small voice in Hebrews 6:1–2.

The six foundations of Hebrews 6 provide a solid rock on which to rebuild the house of faith. The six principles have direct implications for both individual believers and church leaders.

Some church leaders will find it easy to dismiss the contents of this book as an interesting historical footnote about the early days of Christianity. They might not see the need to reconcile their own teaching and their own churches with the pattern offered by the apostles. They might not see much value in implementing the elementary principles—especially if it means challenging conventional norms.

Other leaders might recognize the basic principles of Hebrews 6:1–2 as the foundations of authentic Christianity and immediately set to work realigning their teaching and reeducating their flocks. These will need to look to Messianic Judaism for resources and for direction.

I hope that, at the very least, the Messianic Jewish movement will recognize the need to build upon her own foundations. It bothers me when I see Messianic Jews in the modern Messianic Jewish movement who seem to be more interested in sociology and cultural relevance within the Jewish world than they are in taking hold of their inheritance as the sons and daughters of the prophets, the wardens of the Scriptures, and the inheritors of the promises. In the past, Messianic Judaism has been too distracted by Jewish evangelism efforts to pay much attention to anything other than evangelism. On our current trajectory of bending to accommodate social norms and substituting Torah observance with academic sophistry on the one hand or charismatic song and dance on the other, it will not be long until Messianic congregations will be among the most liberal and secularized of all bodies of faith. If that's where we are going, one must wonder, was there ever any point at all? Maybe we need to go back to catechism class with the apostles.

THE FOUNDATION OF REPENTANCE

The foundation of repentance starts with oneself, not with others. Have we sincerely repented from practicing those things that the Bible forbids and from neglecting those things that the Bible commands? Do we have un-renounced sin in our lives that creates obstacles between us and God? If so, we need to repent. We must not cheapen grace to pardon our own iniquity. We need to quit making excuses for ourselves. Jesus is either Lord of our lives, or he is not, and so long as we refuse to repent, turn from sin, and submit to his Word, he is not. Such a person builds his house on the sand, because he hears the Master's words but does not do them.

The foundation of repentance requires leaders and teachers to present the gospel in terms of biblical absolutes. We must reintroduce wrong and right into our conversation with the non-believer. This does not mean that we should go about condemning people for their sins and shortcomings. We are not in a position to judge anyone. At the same time, we must not allow the cultural preference for an easy, no-commitment, money-back-guaranteed gospel to influence us. The biblical gospel begins with a no-nonsense call for repentance. Jesus hung out with sinners, fallen women, and tax collectors in order to persuade them to repent from their sinful ways. He did not endorse their sinful lifestyles or coddle them with comforting words about God accepting them just as they were. He called on them to repent.

The call to repent, however, has no meaning without a solid standard of wrong and right. Postmodern relativism provides no basis for repentance, since in its framework nothing can be declared to be absolutely right or absolutely wrong, and all behaviors are reduced to a matter of personal preferences and lifestyle choices. Without the solid ground of God's unchanging absolutes beneath our feet (that is, the Torah), we cannot even begin to present the authentic gospel. If Messianic Judaism (or Christianity for that matter) wants to present the gospel, it needs to first affirm the unbending authority of God's law. A theology that teaches that Christ has abolished the Torah effectively neuters the gospel message.

FAITH TOWARD GOD

The foundation of faith toward God implies that we need to exercise the type of faith toward God that Jesus did. On a personal level, this requires much more than an intellectual assent to creed and doctrine. Faith toward God cultivates the fear of the LORD—the unwavering conviction that God is just, that he punishes sin, and that he rewards righteousness. "Do not be deceived: God is not mocked, for whatever one sows, that will he also reap" (Galatians 6:7). God is not distant, remote, uninterested, and uninvolved in our affairs.

Moreover, this faith toward God must be defined by the revelation of God through Jesus. As a fundamental teaching of the Messiah, faith toward God must be the kind of faith in God that Jesus taught, and it cannot be separated from our allegiance to Jesus. This is the confession of faith for which the first-century believers were willing to die and did die. The type of faith that the writer of the book of Hebrews had in mind—"the assurance of things hoped for, the conviction of things not seen"— is the same faith that inspired the biblical heroes he lists in Hebrews 11 to persevere despite adversity and disappointment. If you feel lukewarm in your commitment to God or your commitment to the Messiah, unwilling to completely commit your whole life to him, you are short on faith toward God and need to pray, "I believe, help me with my unbelief" (Mark 9:24).

Leaders and teachers need to present a faith in God that goes beyond the faith of those shuddering demons in James 2:19. We need to cultivate a vitality in faith that results in good works and deeds: "For as the body apart from the spirit is dead, so also faith apart from works is dead" (James 2:26).

Faith toward God includes confidence in his mercy and in the merit of our Master's suffering. This faith proclaims the forgiveness of sins and hope for eternal life in Jesus' name, but it demands more than just believing in him for the forgiveness of our sins. A gospel message that proclaims faith toward God teaches confidence in God's sovereignty and in His goodness. It teaches tenacity in prayer, perseverance in suffering, and quiet optimism in the face of disappointment. It does not consist of dogmatic formulas; it does not consist of a theological checklist to which a person must assent in order to be guaranteed salvation. When we present the gospel to people, we must resist the urge to oversimplify the depth and the demands of faith.

INSTRUCTION ABOUT WASHINGS

The foundation of instruction about washings has little to do with the mode of baptism and much to do with the preparation for baptism. Chances are that most people who self-identify as Christians or Messianic believers were never required to learn the Master's teachings prior to immersion. Most likely, they needed to affirm a few doctrinal points about Jesus, his divine nature, his death for sins, eternal life, and so forth, but most were probably not required to even read through the Sermon on the Mount. A person who has become a disciple without first counting the cost, without first learning the demands of discipleship, can be compared to someone who signs a contract without ever looking at the terms and conditions.

If you entered the faith without first receiving the instructions, you need to backtrack and learn the teachings and sayings of the Master. Jesus' teachings in the Gospel of Matthew are a good place to start in order to find out what you have signed up for as his disciple.

The foundation of instruction about washings calls upon leaders and teachers to develop a type of curriculum, a modern *Didache*, so to speak, that succinctly presents the teachings of Jesus and the ethics of the Torah to new believers. Candidates for baptism should be required to learn the demands of discipleship and the instructions of our Master before they agree to take on his yoke. They should be required to learn more about the ethical standards and kingdom values of Jesus and less about the theological dogma of how salvation works. They should be encouraged to seriously count the cost before being pushed into the water.

LAYING ON OF HANDS

The foundation of the laying on of hands looks to previous generations of believers to bless the new generation and welcome them into the school of discipleship. It calls upon us all to respect spiritual leadership and spiritual authorities in our lives. We must humbly submit ourselves to those who have been given the task of shepherding the flock, whether that be one's teacher, pastor, elder, messianic rabbi, or other ecclesiastical office. Too much emphasis has been placed on the individual and his personal salvation and not enough on continuity and connection within the body of Messiah, through which the Spirit of God is imparted.

Congregational leaders could reintroduce the laying on of hands as part of the baptism ceremony. Elders of the community could come around the new disciple, lay hands upon his head, and invoke God's blessings upon the new disciple. They should declare the forgiveness of sins in Jesus' name, earnestly pray for the new believer, and ask God to invest him with a generous measure of the Spirit. In this way, the elders of the community would invest the new believer with a sense of expectation and accountability.

RESURRECTION OF THE DEAD

The foundation of the resurrection of the dead requires us to rethink our eschatology and to reorder our priorities. It calls for us to consider the exceedingly higher value of the kingdom and to seek it all the more earnestly. We are not just passing through this world, we are to be transforming this world, living out the resurrection of Messiah right now as we make the world a better place. We need to steward our bodies, because one day they will be immortal, and they deserve that dignity. We need to steward the planet, because this is the place where the kingdom will take place, not up in heaven.

The doctrine of the resurrection provides people with solid answers and solid hope for a dying world. It changes the emphasis from the incorporeal to the corporeal. Leaders and teachers need to clearly communicate the hope of the resurrection to the potential disciple, and we must present the resurrection as the objective of our faith. Pastors and Bible teachers need to bring this hope, along with the message of the kingdom, to the center of their teachings. A gospel that neither emphasizes the kingdom on Earth nor the literal resurrection of the dead is a gospel "having the appearance of godliness, but denying its power" (2 Timothy 3:5).

ETERNAL JUDGMENT

The foundation of eternal judgment requires us to set the fear of the LORD back in place as the guiding principle for human choices and behaviors. We find it easy to rely on grace and excuse our own sin, self-indulgences, and vices, all the while consoling ourselves with doctrinal assurances that we will not receive any punishment in the hereafter. The doctrine of the final judgment should make us tremble as we consider the awesome prospect of giving an account before the judge and receiving a verdict on our lives. If we properly understand that frightening and inevitable destiny, we will be inspired to cling all the more tightly to the assurances we have found in Jesus' name. The forgiveness of sins becomes not just a theological proposition but a precious and treasured hope.

As pastors, leaders, and teachers present the gospel to the world, we must not backpedal on the doctrine of eternal judgment. We do the world a great disservice if we create the impression that God does not deliver comeuppance after death. At the same time, we should not dangle people over hell in order to persuade them to confess Christ. We should not use the threat of punishment in the afterlife to force people into the kingdom, as if we ourselves already know the verdicts and the outcome of the final judgment. Instead, we should present the eternal judgment as the great reversal in which all that is wrong with the world will be set right. Then the first will be last, and the last will be first; the lowly and downtrodden will be lifted up, and the proud will be brought low. Finally, God's justice will be satisfied, and there will be no dissenters.

ON TO MATURITY

Having completed our short overview of the elementary doctrine of Messiah, are we now prepared to go on to maturity? Are we ready to move on to a more solid diet?

Probably not.

Elementary principles are only the beginning. A catechism presents only the first basic teachings. This is the milk of the Word—just the basic stuff. We have only learned about the foundations, we have not yet laid them. We are like the schoolchild who has only just learned that such a thing as mathematics exists; we have not yet mastered addition and subtraction or our multiplication tables.

To recover the foundations, we need to remove the doctrines, theological assumptions, and ecclesiastical traditions that obscure them. This includes rethinking the theology that says the gospel has canceled the Torah. It requires changing our minds about the true meaning of repentance. It forces us to redefine faith from *what* we believe to *how* we believe.

This recovery cannot happen so long as we allow the sacramental developments around Christian baptism to eclipse the original simple Jewish ritual and the catechetical preparations that the original ritual required. Baptism needs to be understood as an individual's initiation into the life of discipleship, as something not to be entered into haphazardly or without one's full consent.

If we hope to fully recover these ancient foundations, we will need to reintegrate the concept of intergenerational spiritual continuity within the assembly—one generation of disciples investing the next with their identity as disciples of Jesus. This might sound frighteningly hierarchical to many Protestants. The process requires spiritual leaders who are willing to step up to that task, and it requires humility on the part of laymen to submit to spiritual leadership.

Finally, we will be ready to build on the original foundations only after we have reclaimed a proper Messianic Jewish eschatology. We need a solid hope in the resurrection and a firm conviction of the final judgment. Ultimately, our eschatology determines the choices we make in the here and now.

The hard work of rebuilding on top of these foundations still lies ahead, but if we will prayerfully commit ourselves to the task, God will surely strengthen us and grant us success. In the end, the house may be smaller. Our congregations might be smaller. Our appeal to the secular world might be more limited. But beyond any doubt, our communities will be far more biblical, far more kingdom focused, and far more in line with the basic teaching of Jesus.